Lincoln and the Bolts of War

Rolando Avila

R & L Books
United States

ISBN: 069272317X
ISBN-13: 978-0692723173

First Edition

"The old man sits here and wields like a backwoods Jupiter the bolts of war…" (John Hay).

CONTENTS

CHAPTER 1

PRELUDE TO WAR

Lincoln: Forged in the Wilderness

Abraham Lincoln was born in a log cabin on February 12, 1809 near Hodgenville, Kentucky. When he was six years old, Lincoln's family moved to an unsettled wilderness territory near Pigeon Creek, Indiana. It was here, in the "backwoods," that he grew into a young man of twenty.

In the wilderness, there was a lot of hard work to do. Without the use of slave labor, he helped Thomas, his father, clear the land of trees, so that the family could plant crops. He became very handy with the ax, and he used it to split logs lengthwise into rails that he used to build fences. Many years later, when Lincoln ran for president, the Republican Party promoted the rugged image of "Lincoln the Rail-Splitter."

Education was not a priority for people living in the wilderness. As a teenager, Lincoln learned the basics: mathematics, reading, and writing. In total, he had less than one year of formal education, which he received at a local school house. However, he had a keen and inquiring mind. Lincoln was not satisfied with his limited education. He read as much as he could. He read the few books that made up the Lincoln home library. He borrowed books from neighbors. He used books to learn grammar and pronunciation. He learned speech presentation techniques. He learned about federal, state, and local laws.

He used memorization as a way to internalize material. His neighbors were amazed at how he could recite long passages from books he had read. Other neighbors recalled how he would recite Sunday church sermons from memory. He practiced his math in notebooks. When no paper was available, he wrote on wooden boards. He practiced his writing by composing poetry. At least one of his poems was published in a local newspaper. He was fascinated by stories. He loved to read them and he loved to tell them. He read stories in the family Bible. He read Aesop's Fables (tales with a moral). He loved to tell jokes, because they helped him cope with the pressures of life. As an adult, he read and recited passages from Shakespeare plays. He also reflected on Shakespeare's lessons on the human condition.

With his life-long practice of self-education, he became a land surveyor, a store clerk, a lawyer, and a politician. Although he built heavily upon a basic educational foundation throughout his entire life, he believed that his self-education was sorely lacking. In his first autobiography he wrote only one word to describe his education: "defective." Colleagues and rivals sometimes underestimated Lincoln because of his "backwoods" background. However, no one underestimated him for very long.

He was forged in the wilderness, and he came to believe that just as his strong mind and hard work had helped him rise beyond his humble beginnings, every man should be allowed to rise as far as his talents and hard work could take him. In this respect, freedom was essential in order for people to achieve their dreams. He wrote in 1859, "We know, Southern men declare that their slaves are better off than hired laborers…. How little they know, whereof they speak…. Free labor has the inspiration of hope…slavery has no hope."

Economy: North and South

Slavery was a part of American history since before the American Revolution. Due to climate and environmental differences, the North relied much less on slavery than the South. In the North, the climate was not conducive to large scale agriculture, because of the cold weather. Consequently, northerner entrepreneurs had to find other ways of making a living, and they primarily focused their efforts in trading, ship building, and fishing. When industrialization made its way from Europe to America, the North became the nation's leader in industry and free labor.

In contrast, the Southern climate was warm and the soil was fertile. As a result, Southerners chose to base their economy on agriculture, which was dependent on slave labor. Tobacco was the first major money maker in the thirteen colonies. But, shortly after the American Revolution the institution of slavery began to die out in the North and to decline in the South. However, the invention of the cotton gin (a machine that was used to easily remove the seeds from the cotton boll) in the 1790s revived slavery in the South. Before the cotton gin was invented, it took one slave about 10 hours to produce one pound of clean cotton fiber. After the invention, slaves were able to produce about 1,000 pounds of cotton a day. Although tobacco and other crops were still grown, Southern entrepreneurs began focusing most of their resources on "King Cotton," because it had become their most profitable crop. By 1860, about four million slaves lived in the U.S. Most of them lived in the South.

Cotton gin

Many people believed that the different environments and different economies had created many competing interests (or sectional differences) in the North and South. One basic difference had to do with the kind of workers that each region employed; free labor in the North and slavery in the South. Many people believed that competing interests were tearing the nation apart. Lincoln disagreed.

He acknowledged the differences, however, he believed that they united the nation. The North needed raw materials (such as cotton) from the South, and the South needed finished goods (factory-made goods) from the North. In other words, each region was dependent on the other. He explained:

> The great variety of…institutions in the states, springing from differences in the soil…and in the climate, are bonds of union…. If they produce in one section of the country what is called for by the wants of another section…they are not matters of discord but bonds of union…

The "Mudsill" Theory and Abolitionists

By the time of the Civil War, slavery had been a part of Southern society for so many generations that it had become ingrained in the Southern culture. Writers and politicians referred to the institutions of slavery as the "mudsill" (or foundation) of Southern society. Even if they had never owned slaves, most Southerners were protective of the institution of slavery, and they were sensitive to anything that threatened their way of life. A perceived insult to Southern honor was commonly regarded as sufficient cause for violence. Southerners saw abolitionists (activists who wanted to get rid of slavery) as a threat to Southern values, and a handful of high profile abolitionists made the anti-slavery movement their life's work.

Lincoln understood that Southerners were protective of the institution of slavery. He wrote in 1859, "The autocrat of all the Russias will resign his crown…sooner than will American masters voluntarily give up their slaves." Lincoln described his personal feelings about slavery in a Chicago speech in 1858, "I have always hated slavery, I think as much as an Abolitionist."

5

Wm. Lloyd Garrison.

William Lloyd Garrison (1805-1879) was one of the most influential figures of the abolitionist movement. During the American Civil War, Garrison edited *The Liberator*, an anti-slavery newspaper. He called the Constitution "a pact with Hell," because it protected slave property. He accused the nation of "legalizing, on an enormous scale…cruelty and murder" against slaves.

I SELL THE SHADOW TO SUPPORT THE
SUBSTANCE.
SOJOURNER TRUTH.

Sojourner Truth (c. 1797-1883), a runaway slave, was one of the most famous African American women activists of the 19th Century. She rejected her slave name and renamed herself "Sojourner Truth," because she traveled the country preaching the "truth" about the evils of slavery and other issues. She once said, "I feel safe in the midst of my enemies, for the truth is all powerful and will prevail." During the war, she met with President Lincoln to ask for permission to aid wounded African American troops, and Lincoln granted her request. Truth inspired many people to support her causes.

Frederick Douglass (1818-1895), a runaway slave, edited an abolitionist newspaper and delivered anti-slavery lectures. In 1845, Douglass wrote his life story (*Narrative of the Life of Frederick Douglass*), which provided a first-hand account of slave life. His story convinced many people of the evils of slavery. During the war, Douglass helped persuade President Lincoln to allow African Americans to serve in the Union army. Douglass believed that military service was a vital step in African Americans earning citizenship rights.

Underground Railroad

The Underground Railroad was a loosely organized network that aided runaway slaves to escape from bondage. It was not really "underground" and it was not a "railroad." It was referred to as "underground," because it was secret, and it was tagged a "railroad," because the network was used to transport slaves. Secrecy was necessary, because the practice of aiding slaves to run away was illegal. Fugitive Slave Laws called for stiff fines and imprisonment for those who stole or aided in the theft of slave property. However, some citizens chose to disobey the slave laws, because they believed that slavery was morally wrong. Some people ran safe houses. Others contributed money to keep the network running. For example, Harriet Beecher Stowe, the author of the famous and influential abolitionist novel, *Uncle Tom's Cabin*, participated in the Underground Railroad in Cincinnati, Ohio, because she was moved by the plight of the fugitive slaves.

The prevailing myth about the Underground railroad is that slaves that traveled through the "rails" were merely "packages" that "conductors" ushered to freedom. However, slaves played much greater roles in their escapes. The network, which was made up of many routes that extended through at least fourteen states, began north of the Mason-Dixon Line. This discouraged most slaves in the Deep South to attempt the long journey north. Very few people, like Harriet Tubman (who was a runaway slave herself), were brave enough to journey into the south to "abduct" slaves. Consequently, most slaves that escaped had to do so out of their own initiative and resourcefulness. Some slaves escaped south to Mexico. However, most slaves that attempted to escape failed, and the total number of slaves that escaped accounted for a small percentage of the total slave population.

LC-USZ62-7816

Harriet Tubman (1823-1913)
nurse, spy and scout

At great risk to herself, **Harriet Tubman** (c. 1820-1913), the "Chief Conductor" of the Underground Railroad and abolitionist, made about nineteen trips into the South to rescue slaves. During the war, she supported the Union cause as a nurse, a spy, and a scout. In 1863, Tubman witnessed the 54th Massachusetts (all African American) regiment's attack on Fort Wagner (depicted in the motion picture, *Glory*), and she tended to the casualties after the battle.

Mexican-American War

In 1846, President James K. Polk went before the U.S. Congress and declared, "American blood has been shed on American soil" by Mexican troops. Polk then asked Congress to declare war against Mexico. Although Congress did not officially declare war, it did approve money for the war. During Lincoln's term in Congress (1847-1849), he opposed the war, because he believed that a U.S. victory would net the U.S. a lot of Southern (slave) territory, which would throw off the nation's balance of political power between free and slave states.

Abraham Lincoln, 1848

As a member of the Whig Party, Lincoln accused Polk of starting a war on false pretences. In this regard, in 1847 Lincoln introduced the "spot resolution" that called for information about the exact spot on which Mexicans had shed American blood. Lincoln's intention was to prove that the blood had been shed only after American troops had invaded Mexican territory. In the face of Manifest Destiny, a strong popular desire for the nation to expand, Lincoln's resolution was unpopular. The war went on in Mexico, and critics nicknamed him "Spotty Lincoln." He was never again elected to Congress. Lincoln spent the next decade practicing law.

The Treaty of Guadalupe Hidalgo, which formally ended the Mexican-American War in 1848, ceded nearly one-third of Mexico's territory to the United States. Furthermore, as part of the agreement, the question of U.S. ownership of Texas was settled. This accounted for more than one million square miles of new Southern (slave) territory added to the nation. Years later, historians identified the Mexican cession as a major long term cause of the American Civil War.

States' Rights versus Federal Authority

During the Constitutional Convention, delegates had wrestled with the issue of state's rights versus federal authority. Some delegates feared that if the federal government were given too much power, it would trample on the rights of the states. Other delegates believed that if too much power was granted to the states, it would lead to the creation of separate self-ruled nation-states instead of a united nation.

In order to secure the necessary votes for the passage of the Constitution, delegates ultimately compromised by creating a system in which powers were shared between the states and the federal government. Ever since that time, both states' rights advocates and proponents of federal authority were able to turn to the Constitution and find support for their respective views on the division of powers.

Another interpretation of the nation's origins also provided state's rights activists with support. Since the Constitution, which claimed the supremacy of federal authority, was adopted to "form a more perfect Union," that implied that the Union already existed before the Constitution was drawn up. When was the U.S. established then and on what principles?

One interpretation was that the Declaration of Independence (1776) gave birth to the nation. According to the Declaration, governments were created to serve the people, and, if a government "becomes destructive of those ends," it is the right of the people to do away with it and create a new one.

Federal Compromises

Political power became much more important as new territories and states were added to the nation, because the balance of political power could determine federal policy on the slave issue. Both the Missouri Compromise (1820) and the Compromise of 1850 were federal attempts to ease rising national tensions. Under the Missouri Compromise, Congress admitted Missouri as a slave state and Maine as a free state in 1820 (bringing the total of states in the Union to 24). This achieved the objective of balancing political power by keeping the number of slave and free states equal (12 slave and 12 free). The Compromise also restricted slavery south of Missouri's southern boundary. However, the balance did not last for long as more states were added to the Union, especially in the South after the Mexican-American War in 1848.

Under the Compromise of 1850, Congress admitted California as a free state and strengthened the Fugitive Slave Act (which made it a crime for slaves to run away and for others to help slaves run away). Slave owners wanted to protect their slave property, and they wanted to discourage others from helping their slaves escape. Unfortunately, the new law was not very effective in that regard. Instead, it increased national tensions. According to historian Larry Gara, "The Fugitive Slave Law resulted in the return of only 200 Negroes. But, by inflaming Northern opinion, it helped bring on the Civil War."

Slave Life

Slave life was usually very unpleasant. According to the law, slaves were property, and slave owners could legally do with their property as they chose. Slaves could be sold at any time, regardless of marriage status. Slave families were often broken up as husbands, wives, and children were sold off. Children were expected to begin working the land at five years of age. Some slaves ran away and were severely punished for it.

> *Slave families were often broken up as husbands, wives, and children were sold off.*

In the South, slaves lived on the bare necessities of food rations to sustain life. Slave cabins were built with dirt floors. When it rained or snowed the dirt floors soaked up water creating a muddy mess. Slave cabins were hot in the summer and cold in the winter. Beds were often made of straw. Cabin life bred diseases including cholera, diarrhea, typhoid, tuberculosis, influenza, and hepatitis.

When Lincoln was in his early twenties, he took on a job of transporting farm produce by flatboat to New Orleans. There he witnessed the sale of slaves in the market place. He was profoundly moved by the experience. Years later, he wrote, "there were…a dozen slaves, shackled together with irons. That sight was a continual torment to me…."

Uncle Tom's Cabin

In 1852, Harriet Beecher Stowe (1811-1896) published a novel titled *Uncle Tom's Cabin*, which became an extremely effective anti-slavery propaganda tool. Stowe portrayed the cruelty of slavery in dramatic detail. The story moved readers more than any intellectual argument against slavery had ever done.

Many people who had never before taken a stand on slavery, became convinced that it was wrong. The book became a best-seller, selling over a million copies worldwide. It is said that Queen Victoria wept after reading it. The drama served to increase the nation's tensions. It is said that years later when President Lincoln met Stowe, he commented, "So you're the little woman who wrote the book that made this Great War?"

American Colonization Society

What should be done to deal with the "problem?" One group sought to solve the "problem," by removing free blacks from the United Sates. In the early 1800s, Reverend Robert Finley (a Presbyterian minister), Francis Scott Key (author of the "Star Spangled Banner"), and others formed the "American Society for Colonizing the Free People of Color in the United States." The organization, which aimed to send freed slaves to Africa (or some other area outside the U.S.), later became much more commonly known as the "American Colonization Society" (ACS). Henry Clay (an extremely influential politician and one of Lincoln's heroes) served as vice president of the ACS. In 1852, Lincoln delivered the eulogy at Clay's funeral in which he praised Clay's support of colonization.

Members of the ACS had different motivations for supporting colonization. Some members believed that free blacks would never be treated as equals in the United States, and that Africa (or some other area outside the U.S.) offered them more opportunities. Other members pushed for colonization to prevent marriages between freed slaves and whites. Others believed that free blacks were a burden on white society.

The ACS benefitted from a lot of political support. For example, former President Thomas Jefferson publically supported the ACS's goal, and President James Madison arranged for its public funding. In the 1820s, free blacks were sent to live in the African nation of Liberia ("Land of the Free"). Settlers found it difficult to fit in. The natives did not speak the same language. Their customs were very different. In fact, the natives hated the new arrivals and they constantly attacked them. The project was expensive to carry out and maintain, and President James Monroe was forced to ask Congress for more money to continue to fund it.

Lincoln recognized the high expense of the project. In 1854 he still held "high hope" for colonization "in the long run," but impossible in the near future due to lack of "surplus shipping and surplus money." Another obstacle was that many free blacks did not wish to leave the land where they were born and raised. In 1862, Lincoln recognized the "unwillingness" of many free blacks to leave due to a desire to "remain within…the country of [their] nativity." However, Lincoln did not abandon colonization as an option until 1864 (one year before his assassination).

Popular Sovereignty and the Kansas-Nebraska Act

In an effort to take some decision-making power from the federal government, Senator Stephen Douglas promoted Popular Sovereignty (the idea that states and territories should be able to decide for themselves whether to allow slavery). Douglas' idea was so popular that it led to the passage of the Kansas-Nebraska Act in 1854. The new federal law gave the residents of the Kansas and Nebraska territories the right to decide for themselves what to do about slavery within their borders. The experiment was a disaster. Tensions exploded into violence in "Bleeding Kansas" as abolitionists (like John Brown) waged war on slave holders.

The passage of the Kansas-Nebraska Act got Lincoln's attention. In fact, he was "aroused…as he had never been before" by the significance of the law, which could theoretically lead to slavery in even northern states. He immediately reentered politics.

"Bully" Brooks Beats Sumner

On May 22, 1856, Representative Preston Brooks brutally beat Senator Charles Sumner with his walking cane on the floor of the U.S. Congress. According to reports, Brooks' attack was in retaliation for an anti-slavery speech that Sumner had delivered two days earlier. Sumner never fully recovered from the attack.

After news of the assault reached the South, some Southerners sent Brooks new canes as a show of support. The event highlighted the growing tensions between the North and the South and between anti-slavery and slavery factions. Members of Congress began carrying knives and pistols into the seat of government for protection. Things had definitely gotten out of hand, but President James Buchanan did nothing.

Dred Scott Case

In 1857, the U.S. Supreme Court ruled that a slave named Dred Scott, who had lived many years on free soil, could not sue for his freedom, because he had no citizenship rights. Instead, the court said, slaves were legally protected property. Whether slaves lived in slave states (states that allowed slavery) or free states (states that did not allow slavery) did not change their legal status.

The decision declared the Missouri Compromise unconstitutional because, according to the court, Congress did not have the power to interfere with private property in federal territories. The Dred Scott case increased tensions between the North and the South as abolitionists began increasing their efforts and proslavery groups became more entrenched.

Lincoln's "House Divided" Speech

Standing in the Springfield, Illinois statehouse, Abraham Lincoln delivered his "House Divided" speech in 1858. He said:

> A house divided against itself cannot stand. I believe this government cannot endure, permanently half slave and half free. I do not expect the Union to be dissolved – I do not expect the house to fall – but I do expect it will cease to be divided. It will become all one thing or all the other.

In 1861, President Lincoln pledged to the South that he had no intention of abolishing slavery. However, his "House Divided" speech, which he had delivered just three years earlier, made it difficult for them to believe him.

Lincoln-Douglas Debates

During Lincoln's run for a U.S. Senate seat in 1858, he challenged Stephen Douglas, the author of the Kansas-Nebraska Act, to a series of debates on pressing national issues.

Stephen Douglas

During the debates, Lincoln stated that he believed that African Americans were inferior to whites. This appealed to many white voters. The debates were published in national newspapers, and they brought Lincoln national exposure. Lincoln was a moderate in that he did not wish to get rid of slavery. Instead, he wanted to stop slavery from spreading to new areas. Although Lincoln lost the Senate race, his participation in the debates made his views widely known. During the 1860 presidential election, Republicans nominated Lincoln as the Republican candidate for president.

John Brown

John Brown (1800-1859), an abolitionist who was willing to use violence to achieve his goals, planned to capture a federal arsenal, arm his troops, and then wage war on slave owners. Brown believed that freed slaves would rally to his cause, and that his army would grow as he made his way across the country.

In 1859, with the financial support from abolitionists, Brown launched an attack on Harper Ferry, Virginia. That was as far as his plan got. Slaves did not join his army. Instead, the town's people rose up against Brown and trapped him and his men inside the arsenal until federal troops arrived. Lieutenant Colonel Robert E. Lee arrested him. Brown was tried, found guilty of treason, and hanged.

Some of the opposing reactions from Northerners and Southerners revealed the nation's sectionalism, just how wide the gulf between Northern and Southern sentiments and competing interests had grown. Many Southerners praised the execution of a "traitor." While many Northerners praised the actions of a "martyred hero." For example, abolitionist Frederick Douglass summed up his admiration in the following way: "I could live for the slave.

John Brown could die for him."

Perhaps John Brown's greatest historical significance was tied to the reaction of Southern leaders. Fearing a repeat attack by some other radical abolitionist, Southern leaders, for the first time, built up the Southern militia, which became the basis for the Confederate army.

NEGATIVE NO.
LC-USZ62 -2472

John Brown

1860 Presidential Election and Secession

In the two decades preceding the Civil War, the population in the North had exploded. Massive waves of immigrants came from Europe to work in Northern factories. Each immigrant, whether or not he voted, was counted toward representation, but, because of the Three-Fifths Compromise in the United State Constitution, slaves were only counted as three-fifths of a person. The Electoral College was based on population, and as a consequence, the North had a tremendous edge over the South in the 1860 presidential election. Lincoln's nomination by the Republican Party on May 9, 1860, increased the already existing sectional tensions between the North and the South. The *Boston Herald*, a Democratic Newspaper, reported that "the nomination in many respects [was] a strong one, and [would] be difficult to defeat." New Yorker George Tempelton Strong recorded in his diary that, by this point, "Lincoln's election seem[ed] to be conceded." In October, approximately one month before the election, Strong, future Treasurer of the Sanitary Commission, observed that "the Board of Brokers [was] in decided panic. Stocks [were] going down." And the cause was "the anticipation of trouble growing out of Lincoln's election."

In November, 1860, Lincoln did not receive any Southern popular or electoral votes. Not a single person voted for Lincoln in Alabama, Georgia, Florida, Louisiana, Mississippi, South Carolina, Texas, Arkansas, Tennessee, or North Carolina. In fact, Lincoln did not even appear on the ballot in any of these ten states. In the midst of this opposition, Lincoln still arose victorious and became America's sixteenth president. Consequently, many Southerners did not recognize Lincoln as their president. Instead, they saw Lincoln as a leader who had been elected by the North and for the North.

Compromise, which had been a cornerstone in the history of American government, no longer seemed possible. Southerners were alarmed at the election results, because they were concerned that Republicans would pass anti-slavery laws that the South would be politically powerless to stop. How could they allow the North to take their slave property? It would lead to ruin in the South.

Following the presidential election, debates about secession ensued in Southern state legislatures, and most of the slave states voted to seceded from the Union. Before Lincoln was elected in 1860, there were thirty-three states in the Union. By the time of Lincoln's inauguration just five months later, twenty-seven states were left in the Union. In the months following his inauguration, four more states seceded.

Southern leaders sought to set up their own government where they could have a voice and better representation of their interests, values, and culture. The *Alexandria Sentinel* wrote, "We of the South have thus imposed upon us a government outside of ourselves, and founded on a sentiment hostile to our social system." The *Baltimore Daily Republican* assessed, "Abraham Lincoln has been voted for and by the North…but it is very doubtful…he will ever be President of the *United* States."

Some Northerner's felt that Southern states should be allowed to leave the Union if they wished to do so. However, as a lawyer, Lincoln was familiar with legal precedents (legal examples that set a trend). He believed that if he allowed secession to stand, it would grant all states the right to secede. This would mean the eventual political disintegration of the entire Union. Consequently, Lincoln would not allow or recognize secession.

While there were several long-term causes of the war, the event that brought the nation to the brink of war was the secession crisis that occurred in response to the results of the Presidential Election of 1860. The firing on Fort Sumter in 1861 was the immediate spark that ignited the war.

CHAPTER 2

1861

First Inaugural Address

Lincoln stated in his First Inaugural Address (March 4, 1861):

> ...There needs to be no bloodshed or violence; and there shall be none, unless it be forced upon the national authority.... There will be no invasion—no using of force against or among the people anywhere.... The course indicated will be followed...with a view and a hope of a peaceful solution of the national troubles, and the restoration of fraternal sympathies and affections.... In your hands, my dissatisfied fellow countrymen, and not in mine, is the momentous issue of civil war. The government will not assail you. You can have no conflict, without being yourselves the aggressors. You have no oath in Heaven to destroy the government, while I shall have the most solemn one to "preserve, protect and defend" it.

Standoff

South Carolina was the first state to secede (separate) from the United States of America on December 20, 1860. U.S. Army Major Robert Anderson was in command of Fort Sumter, a federal garrison, in Charleston harbor. President-elect Abraham Lincoln expressed his conviction that all federal forts located in Confederate territory were to be held. So, even though South Carolina leaders demanded that Anderson evacuate the fort and leave it under South Carolina's control, Anderson, who was loyal to the Union, would not budge. Confederate troops surrounded the fort, and the standoff lasted for several months.

Fort Sumter

Soon six more southern states followed South Carolina's example. With state legislature approval, Mississippi, Florida, Alabama, Georgia, Louisiana, and Texas joined the ranks of the Confederate States of America. Other southern states were undecided. It was clear to Lincoln that if more states joined the Confederacy, stopping the rebellion would become more difficult.

Dilemma

Expressing his political view, a Radical Republican wrote President Lincoln on April 3, 1861, "give up [Fort] Sumter, Sir, & you are...dead politically....You have got to fight." But, Lincoln did not want to fight. In fact, he did everything he could to avert war. He was faced with a dilemma. If he used military force to protect the fort, as many men from his party demanded, he ran the risk that more southern states would band together against northern aggression. He did not want to lose more states to the Confederate cause. On the other hand, if he did nothing and the fort was lost, he would upset his political supporters, which might restrict his ability to deal with the escalating crisis.

Lincoln's cabinet offered him conflicting advice on several occasions about how to handle the Fort Sumter crisis. Experienced Army General Winfield Scott informed the president, that in his opinion, no military force could secure the fort, and he recommended evacuation. Meanwhile letter writers and White House visitors continued to advise Lincoln to hold the fort, which, due to the ongoing press coverage, had become a national symbol of federal authority by this point.

Lincoln trusted Scott's military expertise, and he considered the real possibility of a military defeat and its consequences. A Confederate military victory at Fort Sumter, with the North as the aggressor, could give the Confederacy the upper hand internationally. Ultimately, it could lead to European aid to the South and, perhaps, even encourage Europe to recognize the Confederacy as a real and independent nation.

Confederate Stand

Confederate leaders took a stand. They felt that a federal fort in their state would remain a constant military threat to them and would contradict their claim of independence. Anderson's supplies were running out, and he would be forced to evacuate if he was not resupplied soon; Confederates were counting on it. Unknowingly, South Carolina Governor Francis W. Pickens provided Lincoln with a course of action. As a threat, Pickens informed one of Lincoln's representatives that Confederate troops would fire on any sign of a U.S. warship or on any attempt to resupply the fort. Only a steamer would be allowed to peacefully enter the harbor to transport the men out of the fort.

Abraham Lincoln's Strategy

There, Lincoln realized, was the solution. What if the Confederacy fired first? This would show all the states and all foreign powers that the North was not the aggressor. In spite of his cabinet's objections, Lincoln made preparations for a peaceful supply mission. Furthermore, he sent word to Pickens that he would send a supply ship that would not fire unless fired upon. His strategy was in line with the message in his First Inaugural Address in which he assured the South that there would be no war unless the South started one.

Abraham Lincoln, 1861

> *"The old man sits here and wields like a backwoods Jupiter the bolts of war...."*

The Backwoods Jupiter

The fate of the nation—whether it would be divided into two separate nations or preserved as one united nation—would be determined during Lincoln's presidency, and he would have to strategize to keep the nation together. John Hay, Lincoln's personal secretary, once described Lincoln's role in a poetic way: "The old man sits here and wields like a backwoods Jupiter the bolts of war...."

Davis Takes Action

In response, Confederate forces spent three days assembling troops around the harbor. If the Union was successful in resupplying the fort, it would mean humiliation and an important setback for the Confederacy's quest for independence. The South's honor was at stake. In addition, if the Confederates waited until the supply ship reached the fort to fire, they would have to do battle against the fort, the supply ship, and nearby U.S. warships at the same time. There was no way around it, Confederate President Jefferson Davis ordered General Pierre Beauregard, the Confederate commander in Charleston, to capture the fort immediately.

The Spark

On April 12 the Confederates opened fire on the fort. The event was the spark that ignited the American Civil

War. Even though the continuous bombardment lasted for 34 hours, the U.S. warships stationed outside of Charleston Harbor made no attempt to enter the harbor and render aid. Not even the supply ship had reached the fort before the attack began. The fort was left to fend for itself, and Anderson surrendered by raising a white flag.

Ironically, the Union defeat achieved Lincoln's plan. The defeat unified the North against the rebels, because,

Confederate President Jefferson Davis

most Northerners felt that the war had begun due to Confederate aggression. Orville H. Browning, Illinois Senator and a close Lincoln friend, recorded in his diary that Lincoln "himself conceived the idea, and proposed sending supplies, without an attempt to reinforce giving notice of the fact to Gov. Pickins of S.C." According to Browning, "the plan succeeded. [The South] attacked Sumter--it fell, and thus, did more service than it otherwise could." Browning was impressed with how Lincoln proved to the seceding states, and to the world, that there would be no war unless it was brought about by the South. Not reinforcing the fort may have seemed like a poor military strategy on Lincoln's part, but it was an evident master stroke, because, by placing the Confederacy in the role of the aggressor, it united Union support against the rebels.

Mobilizing for War

Unfortunately, after the firing on Fort Sumter, four more southern states joined the Confederacy: Virginia, Arkansas, Tennessee, and North Carolina. The number of succeeded states had gone from one to seven and now eleven. Lincoln now had to contend with a much greater military opponent. In addition, he could not afford to lose any more states to the Confederacy.

The headline in the *Charleston Mercury* read: "The Union is Dissolved!" The Confederacy established its capital in Richmond, Virginia, and Davis proclaimed, "All that we ask is to be let alone." But Lincoln would not comply with his request. Lincoln never wavered from his conviction that he had to restore the Union.

After Fort Sumter, Lincoln knew that he had to prepare for war. "The White House is turned into barracks," wrote John Hay, Lincoln's secretary, in his diary on April 18, 1861. "All day the notes of preparation have been heard at the public buildings and Armories." Lines were being drawn. Lincoln offered command of the Union

Army to Robert E. Lee, but Lee declined the honor and went home to fight for the Southern cause. Lee explained, "Save in defense of my native state, I have no desire again to draw a sword." Two days after the surrender of Fort Sumter, Lincoln called for 75,000 three month volunteers from the states to protect Washington. At this point in time, Lincoln, or almost anybody else, did not believe that the rebellion would last longer than 90 days. Lincoln also ordered Congress to meet in special session in three months (on July 4, 1861). In the next few days, troops began marching into Washington.

On April 19, Baltimore Mayor George W. Brown informed Lincoln by letter "that it [was] not possible for more soldiers to pass through Baltimore unless they fight their way at every step." Later that day, Lincoln received a telegram informing him that the 6th Massachusetts Infantry was attacked by a Baltimore mob as it passed through the city. About four soldiers and nine citizens were killed in the struggle. On April 22, a committee of 50 representatives from Baltimore met with Lincoln at the White House and requested that no more troops be allowed to cross through Maryland. A frustrated Lincoln replied, "Our men are not moles, and can't dig under the earth; they are not birds, and can't fly through the air. There is no way but to march across, and that they must do." The next day, Lincoln paced the floor of the White House as he awaited more troops to arrive for the defense of the Washington, D.C. Lincoln wrote a friend, "I do say the sole purpose of bringing troops here is to defend this capital...I have no purpose to invade Virginia or any other State, but I do not mean to let them invade us without striking back."

Opposing View Points

Davis' Argument

Davis delivered a speech shortly after the Fort Sumter bombardment (later included in his book, *The Rise and Fall of the Confederate Government*, 1881) in which he explained that he could not allow the fort to be resupplied, because it would mean maintaining a threat to the Confederacy. According to Davis, Lincoln had left him no choice, and, therefore, Lincoln was to blame for staring the war. Davis explained:

The attempt to represent us as the *aggressors* in the conflict which ensued is as unfounded as the complaint made by the wolf against the lamb in the familiar fable. He who makes the assault is not necessarily he that strikes the first blow or fires the first gun. To have awaited further strengthening of their position by land and naval forces, with hostile purpose now declared, for the sake of having them "fire the first gun," would have been as unwise as it would be to hesitate to strike down the arm of the assailant, who levels a deadly weapon at one's breast, until he has actually fired.

Lincoln's Argument

In Lincoln's view, it was his duty to keep the Union whole, and he would carry out that duty peacefully unless the Confederacy resorted to violence. According to Lincoln, the war was caused by the South, because they chose to use violence to break up the Union. Lincoln explained:

Both parties [the Union and the Confederacy] deprecated [were against] war; but one of them [the Confederacy] would make war rather than let the nation survive; and the other [the Union] would accept war rather than let it perish. And war came.

Days later, Lincoln told a Baltimore reporter, "I have desired as sincerely as any man—I sometimes think more than any other man—that our present difficulties might be settled without the shedding of blood." On April 27, Lincoln ordered the suspension of citizen civil liberties along troop movement lines between Philadelphia and Washington. On May 4, a special Maryland Legislative Committee formally protested military occupation of the state. Furthermore, they asked Lincoln to bring an end to the war by recognizing the Confederacy as an independent nation. Lincoln rebuked them.

In May, Lincoln ordered an increase of the regular army by 22,714 men. He also called for 42,034 more volunteers and for the enlistment of 18,000 seamen. His immediate goal was to enlarge the army to 156,861 men and the navy to 25,000 seamen. However, some governors sent fewer men than Lincoln had ordered from each state. New York was one of the most heavily populated states, and it fell short in meeting the state quota. As a consequence, Lincoln ordered New York Governor Edwin D. Morgan to the White House. Lincoln wrote Morgan, "I wish to see you face to face to clear these difficulties about forwarding troops from New York." Morgan intensified his recruitment efforts.

Lincoln Appointment of Generals

From the beginning of the war, Lincoln was confronted with a divided North. Some Northerners wanted to punish the South for treason. Others were content with avoiding war by letting the South go. A review of Lincoln's incoming mail reveals that few of the letter writers wanted to fight in the Civil War. One letter writer poetically expressed his views in the following way: "Abraham Lincoln. Put off your shoes now from your feet, for the ground whereon you stand is holy. You stand on the hearts of widows and orphans…and the voice of their wailing goes up to God this day…."

In order to address the lack of Northern support for the war effort, from early on in the war, Lincoln began the much criticized practiced of appointing political generals. When it came to appointing generals, Lincoln cared a great deal about their party and ethnic affiliations, because these affiliations provided Lincoln a way to balance the interests. Lincoln felt that this balancing act was necessary to keep the army from joining the Radical Republicans or other groups who he perceived to stray from his grand strategy of reunification. His political appointments also did a great deal for his popularity with the soldiers.

Regardless of party affiliation, once Lincoln had appointed a general, he would support him as long as he was winning battles. The opposite was also true. He fired generals from both parties. Lincoln once gave a young German a commission in a cavalry regiment, and the happy youth, in an effort to prove that he deserved the honor, saw fit to inform the president that he belonged to an old noble German family. Lincoln responded, "Oh, never mind that, you will not find that to be an obstacle to your advancement."

During a meeting with Secretary of War Edwin Stanton, Lincoln expressed a desire to award a generalship to a German American in order to satisfy the large German ethnic constituency in the North. Looking over the list of German Americans, Lincoln was struck by the name of Alexander Schimelfenning. When Stanton pointed out to Lincoln that there were many other German Americans who were better qualified, Lincoln insisted on Schimmelfenning. "The very man!," he said. "His name will make up for any difference there may be." Lincoln laughed and walked away repeating the name "Schimmelfenning."

Some of Lincoln's political generals included Carl Schurz, Nathaniel Banks, Benjamin Butler, Robert Toombs, Henry Wise, Lew Wallace, George B. McClellan, U.S. Grant, and William T. Sherman. Some political generals proved to be very effective in fighting Lincoln's kind of war. Others did not. He sustained the successful generals, and he removed all those that were unsuccessful. All political generals formed an effective part of Lincoln's grand strategy, because it was an effective way of uniting the North behind the war effort.

Lincoln's Military Background

Speaking before Congress in 1848, Lincoln disparaged his own military experience. "By the way, Mr. Speaker," Lincoln began:

> Did you know I am a military hero?" Yes, sir, in the days of the Black Hawk war, I...bled, and came away.... It is quite certain I did not break my sword, for I had none to break; but I bent a musket pretty badly on one occasion....by accident.... I had a good many bloody struggles with the mosquitoes....

If this anecdote is any indication of Lincoln's true experience in the war, it is safe to say that when Lincoln took office he had no military experience whatsoever. Lincoln did, however, take his role as Commander-in-Chief very seriously, and he quickly set out to banish his ignorance.

Lincoln Learns

Lincoln borrowed military books from the Library of Congress and studied intensively. He asked his generals and cabinet members questions on military matters. He kept abreast of minute details of ongoing military movements. Generals were sometimes surprised or even uncomfortable with Lincoln's familiarity with their military operations, because it made them feel accountable. Lincoln spent much of his time at the War Department's telegraph office receiving messages, sending messages, reviewing battlefield maps, and designing military plans. He enjoyed devising and presenting military plans to generals who were recognized experts in the field. He visited the front on several occasions in order to interview generals and to get a first hand perspective on events. Lincoln's military knowledge grew steadily over time. Historian T. Harry Williams assessed:

> Abraham Lincoln was a great war president.... With no knowledge of the theory of war, no experience in war, and no technical training, Lincoln, by the power of this mind, became a fine strategist. He was a better natural strategists than were most of the trained soldiers. He saw the big picture of the war from the start. The policy of the government was to restore the Union.... His strategic thinking was sound and for a rank amateur astonishingly good.

John Hay, Lincoln's personal secretary, wrote, "Some well-meaning newspaper advise[d] the President to keep his fingers out of the military pie.... The truth is, if he did, the pie would be a sorry mess...."

Union Advantages

By comparison, the mostly agrarian South faced off with a Northern industrial giant. About 92% of all factories were in the North. This meant that the North could more easily supply Union troops with war materials than the South. About 71% of the population was in the North. Compared to the South, the North had more people that could support the war on the home front and the war front. About 72% of all railroad tracks were located in the

North. This gave the Union an advantage with the transport of troops, horses, guns, food and many other supplies.

Comparing Civil War Resources

Manufactured goods
> North: 92%
> South: 8%

Population
> North: 71%
> South: 29% (1/3 of the population was enslaved)

Railroad Mileage
> North: 72%
> South: 28%

(U.S. Bureau of the Census. (1975). *Historical Statistics of the United States, Colonial Times to 1970, Bicentennial Edition.* Washington, DC.)

Most of the mineral deposits were in the North, which were needed to run the factories and to make war materials like explosives. In addition, the North was in command of almost all of the naval ships. This superiority gave the Union the ability to blockade Southern ports. At General Winfield Scott's suggestion, Lincoln used a blockade as a long-term military strategy for the entire duration of the war.

Confederate Major Objectives

From the beginning of the war, Confederate leaders had three main objectives. First, they wanted to keep slavery. In fact, the Confederate Constitution was very similar to the U.S. Constitution with one glaring exception: the

Confederate Constitution specifically mentioned that the institution of slavery was protected by law. Second, they wanted to get and keep their independence. However, in order to achieve these first two objectives, they had to win the war, and they had to do it quickly before they ran out of men and supplies.

Confederate leaders knew that they were out-gunned and out-manned: They were literally out-matched. They knew that, on their own, they had no hope of winning a long war, because their ability to make war would diminish over time. So, their third objective was to try to end the war as quickly as possible by seizing forts and by launching large aggressive attacks against the U.S. capital.

Union Major Objectives

In the early years of the war, Lincoln ran the war by executive order, because Congress was not in session. In fact, only a part of Congress remained after many representatives left the Union. So, Lincoln's major objectives and the Union's major objectives were one in the same. First and foremost, Lincoln wanted to preserve the Union. He wanted to discourage any more states from leaving the Union, and he wanted to convince seceded states to return to the Union.

How was he going to accomplish this objective? Lincoln did not want to alienate the South any more than it already was. Instead, Lincoln wanted to follow a course of action that would convince Southerners that the North and South could still be friends. In the early years of the war, Lincoln avoided destroying a lot of Southern raw materials (like cotton) and railroads. Lincoln hoped for a quick peace, and Southern raw materials were needed in the Northern factories. In like manner, Northern businessmen needed the railroads in place so that they could transport and sell their finished goods to the South.

In 1861 and 1862, Lincoln waged a moderate war against the South. He wanted to keep Southerner destruction and causalities to a minimum, because he did not want to create hatred and distrust between the North and South. He was convinced that an aggressive approach was a mistake, because it might push Southerners away forever.

Anaconda Plan and Strategic Strikes

In June 29, Lincoln called several generals to a meeting to discuss the state of the Union. General Irvin McDowell presented a plan to attack Confederate troops under the leadership of General Beauregard at Bull Run (Manassas). However, General Winfield Scott disagreed.

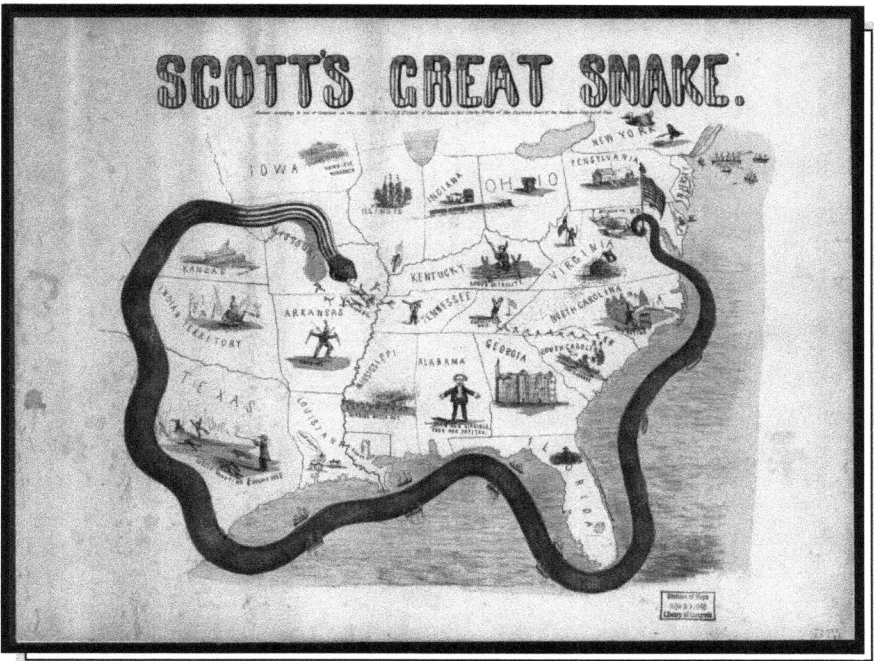

Cartoon map ("Scott's Great Snake") illustrates General Winfield's Scott's plan to blockade Confederate ports.

General Winfield Scott

Scott had been in the army continuously since the War of 1812 and was one of the few commanders in either army who had ever had a field command at the brigade level. By

1861, Scott was old and feeble. Walking was a difficult thing for him to do. However, Lincoln still believed Scott to be his most experienced and best strategically able general.

Scott expressed his regret that Union troops were still not ready for battle. For this reason, Scott proposed a blockade of Southern ports as a way of starving the South into submission. Consequently, even after the South had demonstrated its aggressive stance at Fort Sumter, Lincoln continued a policy of moderation. The Anaconda Plan, suggested by Scott, was a prime example of this kind of limited war strategy. The blockade of Southern ports was intended to isolate the South both economically and diplomatically from Europe. Slowly but surely, the blockade would choke trade and the South's economy would suffer. This economic hardship brought on by isolation, Lincoln believed, would allow cooler heads in the South to prevail and the seceded states would beg for reunification.

Along this same line of reasoning, the limited strategic strikes were intended to either protect the Union from invasion or attack certain points that would weaken the South militarily. In all of these instances, Lincoln wanted to demonstrate to moderate Southerners, Northern Democrats, and foreign diplomats that his was the side of reason and patience. At the president's request, Scott sent Lincoln daily reports on military developments. Concerned with the defense of the U. S. capital, Lincoln often reviewed Union troops and fortifications. The first major threat to the capital came in late July.

First Battle of Bull Run (July 21, 1861)

Just before the First Battle of Bull Run, General McDowell commented to British Reporter William Howard Russell, "I declare I am not quite easy at the idea of having your eye on me, for you have seen so much of European armies, you will, very naturally, think little of us, generals and all." As it turned out, McDowell's comment proved to be correct. Russell was not impressed at all with what he saw at Bull Run on July 21, 1861. The Union's "grand debacle" that day, according to Russell's report, was due to the Union's "crude organization" of its troops. Russell was amazed at the willingness of many volunteers to flee rather than fight. Even at his distant observation post on a hillside, Russell soon found himself "enveloped in the crowd of fugitives." As a direct result of Russell's critical report of the battle, the Union Army no longer allowed him to accompany any further major campaigns. Russell returned to England and wrote a diary of his experiences in America during the first nine months of the war.

Another observer, Lieutenant-Colonel Marcel Victor Paul Camille Ferri-Pisani, Napoleon III's Aid-de-Camp, was also very critical of the lack of dependability of America's crude volunteer troops. That same day, this French visitor wrote that "the results of the battle [were] disastrous and even shameful." He exclaimed that, "the volunteers or militia who fled rather than fight at Bull Run...returned home without worrying in the least about the fate of Washington." Fortunately for the Union, the Confederate troops retreated after the battle.

Lincoln spent most of the day at the War Department telegraph office receiving news and analyzing battlefield maps. He remained awake all night interviewing eyewitnesses of the battle. At sunrise, Lincoln witnessed the retreating army walking by the White House. For the sake of safety, Scott advised Lincoln to send Mary Todd, his wife, and his sons further north. However, Mrs. Lincoln refused to leave her husband's side.

The Confederate victory at First Bull Run (First Battle

of Manassas) convinced Southerners that they had a good chance of winning the war, because it seemed that Northerners did not have the will to fight. Causalities on both sides were in the thousands (4,878 total). After the Union defeat at First Bull Run, Lincoln and Congress took immediate steps to better protect the capital. Union troops built a 37 mile-long defensive ring around Washington consisting of 68 forts. On July 23, two days after Bull Run, Massachusetts Senator Charles Sumner visited with Lincoln to discuss the possibility of emancipating slaves. That same day, Lincoln composed a memorandum on the military policy he wanted his generals to follow.

Lincoln's Bull Run Memorandum

The First Battle of Bull Run was an eye opener for Lincoln. He did not expect the North to lose as badly as it did, and, in an effort to find something positive from a colossal disaster, he took it upon himself to figure out lessons that could be learned from the defeat. Lincoln's "Memoranda of Military Policy Suggested by the Bull Run Defeat" was an attempt to do just that. He ordered the "plan for making the Blockade effective" to be "pushed forward." He ordered that the volunteer forces "be constantly drilled, disciplined, and instructed." He ordered the forces in the West and East to "act," and he ordered the Army to seize and permanently hold Manassas junction so that "an open line from Washington to Manassas" could be utilized.

Clearly, this early memorandum shows that Lincoln had a broad strategic plan for the Union war effort. His zeal to expedite the implementation of the Anaconda Plan was an effort to isolate the South, and render it diplomatically and economically handicapped. His call for disciplined troops shows that he was very much aware of deficiency in this respect. Lincoln's memorandum also shows that he was convinced that the war had to be waged on more than one front at a time, and he was aware of the great importance of railroad transportation.

Generals McClellan and Fremont

Following the First Battle of Bull Run campaign, Lincoln took steps to insure the training of the ill-prepared troops. He summoned General George B. McClellan ("Young Napoleon") to Washington. The president highly valued General McClellan's talent for organization, and assigned him the task of organizing the raw and undisciplined troops into an efficient fighting machine. On July 27, Lincoln placed McClellan (also nicknamed "Little Mac") in command of all troops stationed at the capital, and he asked him to draw up a grand military strategy for the entire war.

McClellan's plan called for 273,000 troops to be used in crushing the Confederate capital in Richmond, Virginia. However, McClellan's massive operation was not practical given the Union's existing much lower troop numbers. Even if the troops were made available, using all of them to launch an attack in one focal point would leave Washington unprotected. Lincoln could never approve of such a plan.

After McClellan fulfilled his assignment to train the Army of the Potomac to Lincoln's satisfaction, Lincoln placed McClellan in command of military operations in the East, and he appointed General John C. Fremont ("the Pathfinder") to lead troops in the West. To Lincoln's disappointment, Fremont made a terrible mistake. He acted beyond his military operational capacity by formulating government policy. Without consulting Lincoln, in August Fremont began freeing the slaves of any people he considered to be resisting the will of the government.

General George B. McClellan

Lincoln had made a commitment to leave slavery untouched, because he did not want to alienate the loyal slave-holding border states (Union states located on the northern border of the Confederacy). The war, Lincoln insisted, was being waged to save the Union. Slavery had nothing to do with it. He ordered Fremont to stop interfering with slavery, and Fremont obeyed. Due to this serious blunder, Lincoln began to doubt Fremont's judgment. However,

Lincoln was willing to forgive and forget the error if Fremont would give the Union some important victories. Fremont failed to do so, and Lincoln removed Fremont from command in November.

That same month, McClellan began pushing for Scott's removal. Scott, the hero of the Mexican-American War who was nearly 75 years old, weighed about 300 pounds and became dizzy upon standing. Detractors gave "Old Fuss and Feathers," the new nickname of "Old Fat and Feeble." Scott's critics equated his physical problems with mental weakness. Scott resigned and Lincoln placed McClellan in command of the entire Union Army in November.

The *Trent* Affair

The South was aware that Europe needed cotton, and it used this as a bargaining chip. The South's appeal to France for recognition, however, was unsuccessful, because Napoleon III could not afford to wage war against the Union army at a time when Prussia was exhibiting an "unfriendly attitude" toward France. Consequently, the South sent two ministers to Britain to try to encourage recognition. After running the blockade, the two men arrived in Havana and were boarded on a British steamer, the *Trent*. The *Trent*, however, did not escape the Union Navy.

On November 8, 1861, the ship was captured and boarded by the flamboyant Charles Wilkes, who arrested the Confederate officials and ordered them confined as prisoners of war. Although the *Trent* was not damaged and Wilkes allowed the ship to go on its way, British national honor was severely bruised. This series of events set off the North's first major diplomatic crisis, and the Union found itself on the brink of war. In preparation, Great

Britain quickly sent eleven thousand troops to Canada, got the Navy ready, and demanded a release of the two prisoners and a formal apology.

Although Great Britain really did not want war, the British "could not allow its flag to be insulted" in this way. Eventually, the North backed down and the crisis was resolved peacefully with an apology. The Southern ministers were released and allowed to proceed to Britain. Lincoln affirmed that, under the circumstances, this was the best course of action. He said, "One war at a time." As 1861 came to a close, Lincoln made plans for a Union military offensive.

CHAPTER 3

1862

Lincoln Plans and Orders an Offensive

After Lincoln was satisfied that the Army of the Potomac was ready, he ordered McClellan to launch an offensive against the South. Lincoln's plan called for McClellan to move the Army of the Potomac "directly to a point on the Railroad South West of Manassas." Lincoln's plan called for quickly transporting a superior number of troops on the railway and destroying a smaller army. After the defeat at the First Battle of Bull Run, Lincoln knew that the Union desperately needed a victory in order to maintain support for the war effort of reunification.

McClellan strongly disagreed with Lincoln's plan and preferred a Peninsula approach with the object of capturing the Confederate capital at Richmond. Lincoln wrote McClellan a letter listing his objections to McClellan's plan. "Does not your plan involve a greatly larger expenditure of time...than mine?," asked Lincoln.

Lincoln's Letter Outlining Military Strategy

On January 13, 1862, Lincoln sent copies of a letter to both General Don C. Buell and General Henry W. Halleck in which he expressed his view of the best general operational military strategy that should be followed:

> In the midst of my many cares....I state my general idea of this war to be that we have the *greater* numbers, and the enemy has the *greater* facility of concentrated forces upon points of collision; that we must fail, unless we can find some way of making *our* advantage an over-match for his, and that this can only be done by menacing him with superior forces at *different* points, at the *same* time; so that we can safely attack, one, or both, if he makes no change; and if he *weakens* one to *strengthen* the other, forbear to attack the strengthened one, but seize, and hold the weakened one, gaining so much.

Lincoln's letter shows that he was aware of the great advantage that numbers gave the North over the South. He once commented to his personal secretary William O. Stoddard that the war was just a matter of "arithmetic." In Lincoln's opinion, if big battles were "fought over again, every day, through a week of days...the army under [General Robert E.] Lee would be wiped out to its last man...[and] the war would be over...." Stoddard concluded that "no general yet found [could] face the arithmetic, but the end of the war [would] be at hand when he [should] be discovered."

The letter also illustrates Lincoln's departure from Baron Antoin Henry Jomini's principles. While Jomini stressed a concentration of forces for an offensive, Lincoln advocated multiple simultaneous offensives.

As a rule, all West Point graduates were expected to be familiar with Jominian principles. Dennis Hart Mahan, who taught military strategy at West Point for almost fifty years, made sure to include Jomini in his courses. Moreover, Henry W. Halleck's *Elements of Military Art and Science* (1848) was basically a translation of Jomini and was used as a textbook at West Point. It is also worth pointing out that General George B. McClellan, who followed Jominian strategy very closely, was largely unsuccessful. Ulysses S. Grant, on the other hand, who did not do very well at West Point and confessed to never having read Jomini, did very well on the Civil War battlefields. Essentially, while McClellan was to run a protracted war, Grant was to be the general who could face and carry out Lincoln's concept of war "arithmetic."

McClellan's Demotion

Three months after McClellan was appointed as General-in-Chief, he still did not feel ready to launch an offensive. Lincoln grew anxious, and, on January 27, 1862, he issued "General War Order Number 1," which ordered "a general movement of the Land and Naval forces of the United States against the insurgent forces." But, McClellan stuck to his guns, and appealed to Secretary of War Stanton with a twenty-two page letter in which he explained the benefits of his plan to march up the Virginia peninsula to capture the Confederate capital. Such was McClellan's persistence that Lincoln gave in to his plan with the condition that he attack soon and "leave Washington secure." But, Lincoln's order of troop movement had no effect on McClellan. By March 1862, McClellan had still not engaged

General U.S. Grant

the enemy. As a consequence, on March 11, Lincoln demoted him, and left him only with the command of the Army of the Potomac.

Battle of Shiloh (April 6-7, 1862)

In contrast to McClellan, General U.S. Grant was willing to carry out Lincoln's strategic military plan to engage and destroy rebel armies. In April he was victorious against Confederate forces in Shiloh, Tennessee. If the Battle of First Bull Run had given the Confederacy hopes of an easy victory, the events at Shiloh dashed those hopes. Grant's determination during the two-day battle shocked many Southerners. Grant lost about 3,000 more men than the Confederacy, but he won the battle. Total casualties numbered more than 23,000. Grant got Lincoln's attention. While most of Lincoln's generals suffered from what Lincoln called "the slows," Grant was able to win victories without having to ask for more supplies or more men.

McClellan's Peninsula Campaign

McClellan insisted that Lincoln was wrong about the need to destroy rebel armies. According to McClellan, the key to ending the war was to capture the Confederate capital in Richmond. Lincoln reluctantly agreed to allow McClellan to carry out his plan. Undoubtedly, Lincoln preferred McClellan's action over McClellan's inaction.

McClellan moved his massive army by water on the Chesapeake Bay to the tip of the Virginia Peninsula and then began to march toward Richmond. In this way, McClellan's flanks were protected by the York and the James Rivers. Unfortunately for McClellan, hard rains began falling which created mud that considerably slowed his advance.

On June 4, 1862, McClellan sent Lincoln a telegram in which he described the rainy conditions. "Terrible rain storm during the night and morning--not yet cleared off," wrote McClellan, "Chickahominy [River] flooded, bridges in bad condition....[so] I have to be very cautious now." Lincoln acknowledged the "continuous rains" that McClellan had to deal with and warned him to make sure that the "line of communication" was not cut because of it.

Two weeks later, McClellan wrote Lincoln telling him that some ten thousand troops were being sent out of Richmond to reinforce General Stonewall Jackson. Lincoln wrote back telling McClellan that his information was correct, for it had been corroborated by a dispatch from General Rufus King. The next day, Lincoln wrote McClellan again expressing his gratitude and his views. "If large reenforcements are going from Richmond to Jackson," Lincoln wrote, "it proves one of two things, either that they are very strong at Richmond, or do not mean to defend the place desperately."

Unfortunately for McClellan, it also convinced Lincoln that General Jackson might be preparing for an attack on Washington. As a consequence, Lincoln ordered 23,000 troops away from McClellan and back to protect Washington. The order read: "The President, deeming the force to be left in front of Washington insufficient to insure its safety, has directed the McDowell's army corps should be detached from the forces operating under your immediate direction."

At this point, McClellan completely stopped his forward advance, protested the removal of some of his troops, and made it very clear that he could not continue unless he was reinforced. On April 5, 1862, McClellan wrote Lincoln, "the Enemy are in large force along the front....I beg that you will reconsider the order detaching the first Corps

Major General McClellan

from my Command." One day later, McClellan again repeated his "urgent request" to Lincoln that "his division" be returned to him.

The next day, McClellan appealed to Secretary of War Stanton, and greatly under-estimated his numbers. Lincoln wrote back to McClellan two days later about his under estimate on troop strength. "There is a curious mystery about the *number* of troops now with you," Lincoln wrote, "I...obtained...a statement...from your own returns...making 108,000...with you...[but]...you now say you have but 85,000....How can the discrepancy...be accounted for?" Lincoln ended his letter by telling McClellan that he "must strike a blow," and that "by delay the enemy [would] relatively gain...*fortifications* and *re-enforcements*...." He then repeated that it was "indispensable...that [McClellan] strike a blow." Stressing his will yet a third time, Lincoln reminded him that he "*must act.*"

General George B. McClellan and Mary Ellen, his wife

McClellan wrote Mary Ellen McClellan, his wife, "I have raised an awful row about McDowell's Corps....The President...telegraphed me yesterday that he thought I had better break the enemy's lines at once! I was much tempted to reply that he had better come & do it himself." McClellan failed to take Richmond, and he was recalled to Washington. On July 7, 1862, he wrote Lincoln a letter in which he offered advice on how to run the war. McClellan wrote that "the time has come when the government must determine upon a...military policy covering the whole ground of our national trouble." In essence, McClellan failed to see his slow military movements, which allowed the Confederates ample time to prepare for the attack, as a problem and blamed the campaign's failure on Lincoln's lack of effective military and national leadership.

Second Battle of Bull Run (August 28-30, 1862)

After McClellan failed to capture Richmond, Lincoln made plans for another attempt, but with a different general. Lincoln chose Union Major General John Pope, who had distinguished himself in the Western theater of the war. Lincoln placed Pope in command of the newly formed Army of Virginia and gave him the primary responsibility for launching an attack on Richmond as soon as possible.

However, the Confederacy foiled the plans. Confederate General Thomas Jackson attacked Pope's troops as they passed Warrenton Turnpike. The fighting lasted for several hours on August 28 and continued the next day with heavy casualties on both sides. On August 30, General Robert E. Lee pursued Pope's retreating army. And so, Confederates scored a second major victory at Bull Run.

British Economic Woes and Plans of Recognition

As the war progressed, the Union was able to increase

the effectiveness of the blockade. According to noted Historian Frank L. Owsley, in 1861, only 1 out of every 9 blockade runners were captured before they could safely reach their destination. By 1862, the ratio had increased to 1 out of 7 captured; by 1863, the ratio had again increased to 1 out of 4; by 1864, 1 out of 3 were captured, and by 1865, 1 out of 2 were unable to evade the Unions grip of the Southern coast.

The blockade had made it very difficult for the South to supply Great Britain with cotton that it needed for its textile factories. Due in part to these business interests, after the Battle of Second Bull Run, which ended in a victory for the South, British Prime Minister Lord Palmerston, made cautious plans to recognize the Confederacy with the aim of putting an end to the American hostilities and restoring trade.

In addition, these events on the American battlefields prompted other British government officials to start pushing for mediation. It was felt that the war had gone on long enough and that it was time to end it by giving the South what it wanted--independence.

Lincoln Prepares a Diplomatic Weapon

By mid 1862, Lincoln had realized that a moderate course would not win the war. In July 1862, Congress passed the Militia Act that allowed the use of African Americans as auxiliary and as regular soldiers. Shortly thereafter Congress passed the Second Confiscation Act which allowed for the incorporation of former slaves into the Union Army. In order to blunt the harsh laws Congress was passing, Lincoln announced and issued his own proclamation that put his personal stamp of approval on the matters at hand. Both the Confiscation Act of 1862 and Lincoln's proclamation made a war of conquest unavoidable. Referring to his plans for emancipation, Lincoln remarked to an official of the Interior Department, "the character of the war will be changed....the South is to be destroyed and replaced by new propositions and ideas."

The Union could not afford for the British to aid or recognize the Confederacy, because it would make reunification efforts much more complicated. Lincoln had drafted the Preliminary Emancipation Proclamation before the Second Battle of Bull Run, but he was waiting for a Northern victory before he announced it, in part because he did not want it to seem to the British as if it was merely an act of desperation.

Lincoln was well aware of the very strong British Christian humanitarian movement that had been successful in closing down slavery in other parts of the world. He wished to identify himself with them so that he could gather the necessary support to keep Britain out of the war in spite of current military failures. In this regard, the Proclamation functioned as a diplomatic weapon. The Battle of Antietam would give Lincoln the victory that he was waiting for.

Battle of Antietam (September 17, 1862)

In early September of 1862, the Confederate Army began to march toward Washington. In the face of a Southern attack, Lincoln ordered McClellan to take charge of the Army of the Potomac and defend the capital. Lincoln had doubts about McClellan's disposition to attack, but he had still not lost hope in McClellan's ability to organize an effective defense. Confederate General Robert E. Lee's army crossed the Potomac River north of Washington.

As luck would have it, Union soldiers stumbled on a paper wrapped around a few cigars. On close examination, it was determined that this paper was, in fact, a copy of

General Lee's orders for the campaign. The paper was then forwarded to McClellan. That same day, McClellan wrote Halleck that, in his opinion, the paper which was addressed from Lee to General D. H. Hill and had "accidentally come rushed into [his] hands" was authentic, and it disclosed "some of the plans of the enemy." McClellan boasted to Lincoln that Lee had "made a gross mistake and that he [would] be severely punished for it." McClellan assured Lincoln that he would "catch them in their trap." As a consequence of this definite advantage, Lincoln had great expectations for the coming battle.

Lincoln instructed McClellan not to let Lee "get off without being hurt," and to "destroy the rebel army, if possible." When the two massive armies met at Antietam, the casualties were so high on both sides that both the Northern and the Southern press claimed victory for their own side. The *New York Times*, for example, proclaimed the battle a "Great Victory" for the North. In contrast, the *Richmond Enquirer* wrote that they had the "gratification of being able to announce that the battle resulted in one of the most complete victories" for the South.

In the bloodiest one-day battle of the war, McClellan's army was, in fact, able to stop Lee's army from invading Washington. By the end of the engagement, more than 23,000 casualties were scattered across the battlefield. The human cost had been great. Lee was forced to retreat and McClellan was content with that fact. On September 19, 1862, McClellan wrote Halleck informing him that he could "safely claim a complete victory," because the "enemy [was] driven back into Virginia." Lincoln, however, did not see McClellan's success as a "complete" victory, and told him to pursue the enemy. McClellan answered that his men could not march without shoes and fresh horses. Lincoln was furious. He answered:

Are you not over-cautious when you assume that you cannot do what the enemy is constantly doing? Should you not claim to be at least his equal in prowess and act upon the claim?...It is all easy if our troops march as well as the enemy, and it is unmanly to say they cannot do it.

McClellan responded to Lincoln's harsh words by again informing him that he would not move until re-supplied with clothing, horses, and troops. Lincoln grew more and more impatient with McClellan's failure to pursue and destroy Lee's army.

British Officials Push for Confederate Recognition

Even after the Union victory at Antietam and Lincoln's Preliminary Proclamation, some British politicians continued to push for the recognition of the Confederacy. If the Confederacy became a separate nation, the international power of the United States would be greatly reduced. This seemed like an attractive outcome to some British politicians who were concerned over the issue of the balance of world power. Even though the situation called for diplomatic caution, Chancellor of the Exchequer William E. Gladstone, and extremely influential British politician, delivered a speech at Newcastle-on-Tyne on October 7, 1862 where he stated:

We know quite well that the people of the Northern states have not yet drunk of the cup—they are still trying to hold it far from their lips—which all the rest of the world see they nevertheless must drink of.... There is no doubt that Jefferson Davis and the other leaders of the South have made an army...and they have made...a nation.

Gladstone predicted: "We may anticipate with certainty the success of the Southern States so far as regards their separation from the North."

Preliminary Emancipation Proclamation

Besides functioning as a diplomatic weapon, the Proclamation was also an ultimatum to the South. If Confederate states returned to the Union, they would be allowed to keep their slaves. However, if they did not return to the Union by January 1, 1863, when the Emancipation Proclamation was formalized, they would lose their slaves. Although the U.S. Constitution protected slave property, Lincoln explained that the Constitution gave the president the right to confiscate property in times of rebellion. The war measure Lincoln was enacting also extended to Union states that owned slaves. Union states could also keep their slaves as long as they remained loyal to the Union. The Proclamation also functioned as a weapon of war, because by freeing slaves (the South's labor force) Lincoln would weaken the Confederacy's support system, which would hurt their ability to wage war.

> *"My paramount object in this struggle is to save the Union...."*

The announcement got mixed reviews in the North. Some people thought that the Proclamation went too far. Others thought it did not go far enough. For example, *New York Tribune* editor Horace Greeley complained to Lincoln in an open letter about his uncertainty of the "policy that [Lincoln] seem[ed] to be pursuing." Lincoln responded to Greeley in another open letter in an effort to not "leave any one in doubt." Lincoln explained his purpose behind the Proclamation:

> My paramount object in this struggle is to save the Union, and is not either to save or to destroy slavery. If I could save the Union without freeing any slaves I would do it; and if I could save the Union by freeing some and leaving others alone I would also do that. What I do about slavery, and the colored race, I do because I believe it helps to save the Union....

Lincoln concluded by separating his personal view (his "wish that all men everywhere could be free") from his political agenda ("of official duty" to the nation), which was represented in the Proclamation.

Horace Greeley

The British React to the Preliminary Emancipation Proclamation

The Lincoln administration cared about and followed the British press closely. Secretary Seward sent Lincoln a copy of the *London Spectator* with a brief note. It read, "I send the *London Spectator*...in which I have marked an article which may be worthy of your perusal. You are aware that the *Spectator* is a Journal of...influence." As it turns out, however, much of the British Press remained unimpressed with Lincoln's Proclamation. The *London Spectator*, for example, criticized Lincoln. It said that Lincoln's Proclamation liberated "the enemy's slaves as it would the enemy's cattle, simply to weaken them in the coming conflict...." It continued, "the principle asserted is not that a human being cannot justly own another, but that he cannot own him unless he is loyal to the United States." The *London Punch* also criticized. It depicted the Northern cause as a desperate one. Lincoln's Emancipation plan was seen as "Abe Lincoln's last card."

The British Minister in Washington wrote to Foreign Secretary John Russell that "one of the President's motives," in issuing the Proclamation, "must no doubt have been the expectation that it would change the course of public opinion in England...and secure sufficient sympathy to render intervention impossible." He continued, "there is no pretext of humanity about the Proclamation. It is cold, vindictive, and entirely political. It does not abolish Slavery where it has the power to do so; it protects 'the Institution' for friends and only abolishes it on paper for its enemies." Prime Minister Lord Palmerston called the proclamation "trash." In his opinion, it was "utterly powerless and contemptible."

McClellan's Removal

The North needed victories to keep the British out of the war and to end the war as quickly as possible. After Lincoln had seen to it that McClellan had been equipped with supplies and horses, he wrote, "Is it your purpose not to go into action again until the men now being drafted in the States are incorporated...?" McClellan was insulted by Lincoln's bitter sarcasm.

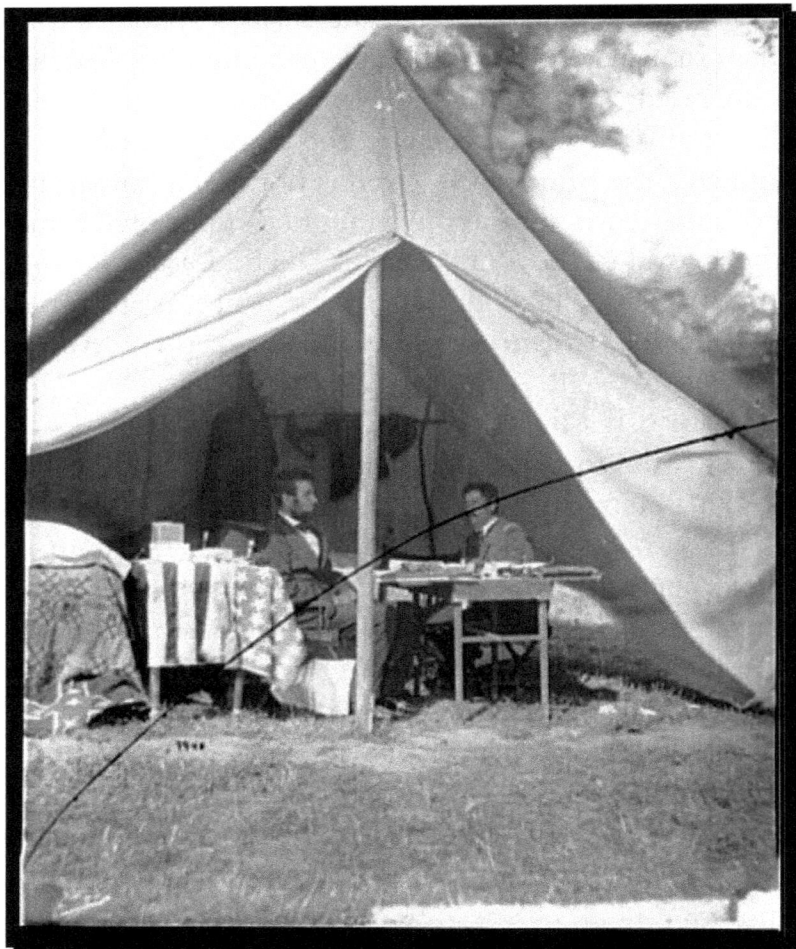

Lincoln & McClellan in a meeting after the Battle of Antietam

Opposing View Points

McClellan's Opinion

McClellan put forth his explanation for his dismissal in his memories, *McClellan's Own Story*, 1887. McClellan, in his attempt to set the record straight, claimed that Lincoln always had the utmost confidence in his abilities. He tells of a secret meeting that took place between Lincoln and himself shortly before his removal from command. According to McClellan, Lincoln assured him that he was satisfied with his performance and that he would stand by him against all critics. In light of this secret meeting, McClellan claims that "whatever changes of mind Mr. Lincoln...underwent may with probability be attributed to...his desire to avoid a rupture with the radical wing of his party...."

Lincoln's Opinion

McClellan's refusal to follow Lincoln's orders to act frustrated Lincoln tremendously. Lincoln was once asked at the White House to assess McClellan's abilities. He responded, "It is doubtless true that he is a good engineer...but he seems to have a special talent for developing a stationary engine." On another occasion, a frustrated Lincoln sent a general telegram that read, "If General McClellan does not want to use the Army, I would like to borrow it for a time, provided I could see how it could be made to do something." On yet another occasion, a frustrated Lincoln called the Army of the Potomac "only McClellan's bodyguard."

McClellan wrote his wife that he was forced, for "the good of the country...to submit to all...from men whom" he knew "to be greatly [his] inferiors socially, intellectually & morally!" McClellan did not cross the Potomac until October 26, which was more than a month after the battle of Antietam. Having demoted McClellan as General-in-Chief in March, on November 7, 1862, Lincoln removed McClellan from command of the Army of the Potomac.

Lincoln Takes Aim at Rebel Armies

Lincoln was, indeed, thrilled with McClellan's ability to defend Washington from invasion. Lincoln knew very well that the capture of Washington would be an enormous military, political, and diplomatic set back. But, Lincoln saw something that McClellan's professional training would not allow him to see. From Antietam on, Lincoln would insist to his generals that the destruction of the rebel armies, and not the occupation of Southern territory, should be their focus.

The Art and Weapons of War

McClellan was, indeed, head and shoulders above everyone else in military knowledge at the time of the Civil War. Unfortunately for McClellan, however, his knowledge was outdated. The Industrial Revolution had changed the nature of warfare. Innovations in the art of war had made old strategies obsolete. While new technologies seemed beyond McClellan's grasp and offended his traditional military tastes, Lincoln developed a strong interest in industrialized warfare, because he did not want a protracted war. He believed that long wars did not go well with democracies.

Lincoln very often got personally involved in the Union's search for new weapons of destruction that would give the North a quicker victory over the South. In 1862, President Lincoln wrote Secretary of War Edwin M. Stanton an executive letter recommending the adoption of a machine gun called the "Rafael Repeater." Lincoln pushed for the development and perfection of small arms, light and heavy artillery, rockets, projectiles, explosives, flame throwers, submarines, naval armor, and land and sea mines. Lincoln was personally "responsible for introducing the machine gun and the breech-loading rifles into the Union Army."

Major General Henry W. Halleck

General-in-Chief Halleck

Lincoln appointed Henry W. Halleck General-in-Chief on July 11, 1862. Halleck saw his role as General-in-Chief much differently than McClellan had. He allowed Lincoln to take full charge of the war effort and merely saw to it that the President's orders were received and carried out by commanders in the field.

Although, realistically, Lincoln functioned as his own General-in-Chief under this arrangement, he did not completely dispense with expert advice. Lincoln and Secretary of War Stanton created an agency known as the Army Board that consisted of the heads of the bureaus of the War department. Ironically, Lincoln had taken McClellan's parting advice to provide an effective military and national leadership very seriously, and, for the next three years, he would step up his efforts to insure Union victory.

More Generals with the Slows

Lincoln was frustrated with generals who never finished preparing for battle, and consequently failed to act. In early October, General Buell informed Lincoln that he had a plan to secure East Tennessee. Weeks passed, but Buell refused to move. Lincoln felt he had waited long enough. He fired Buell and placed General William S. Rosecrans in command of the Cumberland. In November, General Ambrose Burnside proposed a plan to move his army to Fredericksburg and then cross the Rappahannock River and attack Richmond. Lincoln doubted that the plan would succeed, but he was content to see troop movement. A month later, Burnside had still not crossed over the river, and Lee had now positioned his army in Fredericksburg as well. Lincoln had removed McClellan and Buell due to their slowness. Lincoln wondered if he would ever find a general who was faster. He expressed his frustration to a friend: "I am sorry to add that I have seen little since to relieve my fears."

Battle of Fredericksburg (December 11-15, 1862)

In December 1862, 100,000 Union troops led by Major General Burnside engaged 72,497 Confederate troops led by General Robert E. Lee at Fredericksburg. The bloody confrontation resulted in 13,353 Union casualties compared to 4,576 Confederate casualties. On December 15, Burnside retreated. General Lee had gained yet another victory for the South, eliminating any possibility of a Southern surrender by Lincoln's predetermined Proclamation January 1, 1863 deadline.

CHAPTER 4

1863

Lincoln Takes a More Radical Approach to War

By 1863, Lincoln had surely come a long way from his message to Congress, in April 15, 1861, in which he assured the rebels that his object was "to avoid any devastation...destruction...or interference with, property, or any disturbance of peaceful citizens in any part of the country." He had hoped that a moderate approach to war (including hardships brought on by the Anaconda Plan) would be less likely to alienate the rebelling states and more likely to encourage them to peacefully return to the Union. However, by late 1862 (and certainly by early 1863) Lincoln had become convinced that the rebellion could be put down only by complete conquest of the South. According to Lincoln, the Union could no longer afford to pursue "a forbearing" policy. Furthermore, Lincoln reasoned that the Confederates were to blame for the coming doom. Lincoln explained, "They cannot experiment for…years trying to destroy the government, and if they fail still come back into the Union unhurt."

General U.S. Grant recalled that before the war took a more radical approach Union generals were careful "to protect the property of the citizens whose territory [they] invaded." However, eventually the accepted policy became for Union armies to "consume everything that could be used to support or supply armies." Slaves were the South's most valuable property and its most valuable support system. During the early part of his presidency, Lincoln had assured the South that, although he opposed the spread of slavery to new territories, he would not interfere with slavery where it already existed. However, by late 1862, Lincoln had come to see the abolition of slavery as a "military necessity."

In the Emancipation Proclamation, Lincoln proclaimed the slaves, who were held in the rebel South, free because of a "military necessity." "By virtue of the power vested as Commander-in-Chief…in time of actual armed rebellion," wrote Lincoln, "and as a fit and necessary war measure for suppressing said rebellion….I do order and declare that all persons held as slaves within said designated States, and parts of States, are, and henceforward shall be free…." The Proclamation also charged the Executive government with maintaining them free, and receiving them "into the armed service…."

At first, Lincoln had tried gently to push the rebels back into the Union, but when this failed, he took much more drastic measures. In this respect, the Emancipation Proclamation served as a very obvious sign post in Lincoln's change from a limited to an unlimited war strategy. Lincoln effectively used the Emancipation Proclamation as a military and diplomatic weapon which was instrumental in Union victory.

Abraham Lincoln, 1863

British Workingmen React to the Proclamation

As promised in September 1862, the formal Emancipation Proclamation was issued on January 1, 1863. In spite of the initial attitudes of the British press and government, the sentiments of the British workingmen were greatly moved by it. Fueled by abolitionist sentiments, mass meetings of workingmen broke out in Britain in support of the Proclamation. According to the *Anti-Slavery Reporter*, these mass meetings started in January and lasted well into November of 1863.

On January 1, 1863, the *London Daily News* printed a letter of support sent to Lincoln by a group of London workingmen:

> We have watched with the warmest interest the steady advance of your policy along the path of emancipation; and on the eve of the day on which your proclamation of freedom takes effect, we pray God to strengthen your hands, to confirm your noble purpose, and to realize the glorious principle on which our Constitution is founded—the brotherhood, freedom, and equality of all men.

Lincoln wrote back:

> To the workingmen of London.... It seems to have devolved upon [the American people] to test whether a government, established on the principle of human freedom, can be maintained against an effort to build one upon the exclusive foundation of human bondage.

That same day, Mayor Abel Haywood of Manchester, England sent Lincoln a letter with an account of a public meeting he attended. The Manchester working men expressed the following words of support:

As citizens of Manchester...we beg to express our fraternal sentiments...We honor your free States, as a singular, happy abode for the working millions...One thing alone has, in the past, lessened our sympathy with your country and our confidence in it; we mean the ascendancy of politicians who not merely maintained Negro slavery, but desired to extend and root it more firmly. Since we have discerned, however, that the victory of the free North, in the war which has so sorely distressed us as well as afflicted you, will strike off the fetters of the slave, you have attracted our warm and earnest sympathy. We joyfully honor you, as the President...for the many decisive steps towards practically exemplifying our belief in words of your great founders, "All men are created free and equal." Accept our high admiration of your firmness in upholding the proclamation of freedom.

Lincoln responded to the Manchester workingmen on January 19, 1863. He wrote: "I have...been aware that favor or disfavor of foreign nations might have a material influence in enlarging and prolonging the struggle with disloyal men in which the country is engaged...." Lincoln also expressed his desire that the sentiments of the workingmen might also "prevail in the councils of [their] Queen." He continued, "I know and deeply deplore the sufferings which the workingmen at Manchester and in all Europe are called to endure in this crisis." He then proceeded to place all blame for this hardship on the South. He stated that "it [had] been...the attempt to overthrow [the] government, which was built upon the foundation of human rights, and to substitute for it one which should rest exclusively on the basis of human slavery" that brought the war on.

British Political Ramification of the Proclamation

Henry Adams, U.S. minister in England, wrote on January 23, 1863, that the Emancipation Proclamation "has done more for us here than all our former victories and all our diplomacy." In fact, after the proclamation was issued, British "Northern sympathizers outnumbered Southern sympathizers...." But, even though many workingmen had been won over by the Proclamation, the aristocrats, as Charles Francis Adams pointed out, still held to their old notions. Adams wrote on February 27, 1863:

The anti-slavery feeling has been astonishingly revived by the President's proclamation.... It is however to be noted that all this manifestation comes from the working and middle classes. The malevolence of the aristocracy continues to grow just as strong...[and] continue[s] to favor the notion of division and disintegration....

Abraham Lincoln, 1863

Some British officials such as abolitionists John Bright and Richard Cobden were thrilled with the Proclamation and stepped up their arguments against intervention, but most other British government officials, in contrast to many workingmen, remained unimpressed with the Emancipation Proclamation.

Soon after the formal proclamation was issued, an American correspondent for the *New York Times* visited the British Parliament and observed that Earl Derby called the reuniting of the Union "conclusively and absolutely impossible." Lord John Russell held the same opinion and said that the conquest of the South "would be a grievous calamity." Mr. Calthorp, from the Commons, said that he "could not avoid feeling contempt for the Lincoln Administration."

But, even though most of the governing class still favored secession, they could not act on their feelings unless they wished to commit political suicide. For example, the *Manchester Guardian*, a working class newspaper, reported that, due to political pressure from the voting working class, Lord John Russell had adopted a wait-and-see attitude. Russell claimed that the British government was going to remain "neutral" for now but "could not say what circumstances might happen from month to month in the future."

In Parliament, Mr. John A. Roebuck still insisted that if Britain intervened and stopped the war it would put an end to the cotton famine. However, by this point, Roebuck's view was not supported by many other officials in Parliament. Even Lord Palmerston had changed his official stand on aiding the Confederacy. Palmerston explained that he "lamented the sacrifice of life and property in America," but he thought that "at present there was no advantage to be gained by meddling."

Lincoln had intended to use the Emancipation Proclamation as a diplomatic weapon to keep Great Britain out of the American Civil War and to prevent them from recognizing the Confederacy as a sovereign nation. It worked. Although the Emancipation Proclamation did not result in an immediate change in all of British public opinion, it was very effective in accomplishing its intended purpose in a more gradual way. The proclamation had a big effect on the workingmen first, which, in turn, restricted the British government from siding with the, then, unpopular slave-holding South. The South would now have to fend for itself without any hope of European recognition or aid.

> *The Emancipation Proclamation "has done more for us here than all our former victories and all our diplomacy."*

Union Soldiers React to the Proclamation

Many Union soldiers "professed to feel betrayed," by emancipation, because "they were willing to risk their lives [to save the] Union, but not for black freedom." Other Union soldiers, who favored emancipation, were more pragmatic. They believed that "every slave laborer who emancipated himself by coming into Union lines weakened the Confederate war effort," and "also strengthened the Union Army." Some Union soldiers were much more practical than unselfish. They simply liked the idea of African Americans in Union uniforms, because they "might stop bullets otherwise meant for them."

The Proclamation Changes Military Policy

General-in-Chief H. W. Halleck wrote General Ulysses S. Grant informing him that "the character of the war [had] very much changed within the last year." "The North," wrote Halleck, "must conquer the slave oligarchy." The new policy of the government was to "withdraw from the enemy as much productive labor as possible." Halleck explained that "so long as the rebels retain[ed] and employ[ed] their slaves in producing grains...they [could] employ all the whites in the field." Also, the new policy of the government was "to use the Negroes of the South as laborers...cooks...and...a military force....which would afford much relief" to the Union Army. In a convincing tone, Halleck wrote that it was, indeed, "good policy to use them to the very best advantage" of the Union, for "in the hands of the enemy, they [were] used with much effect" against the North. But, to the contrary, in Union hands, they could be used against the rebels.

Halleck realized that using African Americans against the South forfeited any chance of peaceful resolution, writing that, under these new circumstances, "there could be no peace but that which is forced by the sword." He charged General Nathaniel P. Banks with organizing a large force of African American troops.

"Indispensable" African American Troops

Secretary of the Treasury Salmon P. Chase was very much impressed with the effective use of African Americans in the war. Chase informed a friend that General Banks had written to the President informing him that "he could not have taken Port Hudson without his colored recruits." Chase also pointed out that Grant had come to value the "colored regiments" as "indispensable." It has been estimated that more than 180,000 African Americans took part in more than 40 major battles and hundreds of smaller engagements during the last two years of the war. About 68,000 African American soldiers lost their lives in battle. Twenty-three African American soldiers and four African American sailors were awarded the Medal of Honor.

African American Union Troops

"Fighting Joe" Won't Fight

In January of 1863, Lincoln removed Burnside and appointed General Joseph Hooker in command of the Army of the Potomac. "Fighting Joe" Hooker had developed a reputation for aggressiveness on the battlefield. Lincoln did not consult anyone when he made the appointment. Furthermore, Lincoln ordered Hooker to bypass the command system and to report directly to him. Even Halleck was left completely in the dark as to Hooker's plans or the outcome of those plans.

In late January Hooker told a newspaper reporter that, in his opinion, the war would go well for the North only after the North was run by a dictator. Lincoln read the story and informed Hooker, "Only those generals who gain successes can set up dictators. What I ask of you is military success, and I will risk the dictatorship.... Give us victories."

General Joseph Hooker

Lincoln visited Hooker's camp on May 7. Lincoln asked Hooker, "Have you already in your mind a plan wholly or partially formed? If you have, prosecute it without interference from me. If you have not, please inform me, so that I, incompetent as I may be, can try and assist in the formation of some plan for the army." Hooker assured the president that he had a plan, and that he would deliver victory.

Unfortunately, Hooker failed to deliver. After he was appointed to command the Army of the Potomac, he developed the habit of making big plans that would go nowhere, because he would lose his nerve and bring everything to a halt. Lincoln dismissed Hooker in June and appointed General George Mead in his place. For Lincoln, these all too common types of disappointments served to create a stark contrast with Grant's movements. Lincoln told a friend that he was beginning to see General Grant as a rising star.

Grant Rumors

It was common for Lincoln to interview generals before promoting them to important positions. Unfortunately, Grant was far off in the West, too far for Lincoln to meet with him. Lincoln had heard rumors that Grant had a drinking problem, and that his drinking had affected his leadership during crucial moments. In March, Lincoln sent Charles A. Dana (former New York *Tribune* reporter) to Grant's camp to observe the general on a daily basis. The next month, three other observers arrived. For five months, Dana sent favorable reports back to Washington. The reports convinced Lincoln that the rumors about Grant were not true.

Battle of Gettysburg (July 1-3, 1863)

In the summer of 1863, General Robert E. Lee marched his troops across the Potomac River into Maryland. His ultimate plan was to enter Pennsylvania and then attack Washington, D.C., but he was forced to resupply before proceeding. Reports had come in of the existence of a storehouse of shoes in a small town near Gettysburg, Pennsylvania. Confederate command ordered scouts to comb the area looking for shoes and other supplies. To everyone's surprise, the scouts stumbled upon thousands of Union troops in the area.

After the scouts reported back, Lee made preparations to launch an offensive. On the other hand, Union General Mead concentrated on positioning his men in good defensive positions. On July 1, the bloodiest battle of the Civil War began. After the first day of fighting, more than 12,000 men had been lost, but there was no conclusive winner. Both sides knew that the fighting would continue the next day. On the third day, Confederate troops made an unprotected march directly into Union fire ("Pickett's Charge"). In response, the Union mowed down about 5,000 Confederate troops in the space of about 90 minutes. When Lee asked General George Pickett to prepare for a possible Union counter attack, Pickett replied, "General Lee, I have no division now."

Lee ordered his troops to retreated and blamed himself for the defeat. Depressed, Lee offered Jefferson Davis his resignation, but Davis refused to accept it. Consequently, Lee continued to fight until the end of the war, but the Confederacy would never again come as close to the U.S. capital or have the ability to launch such as massive attack. The Battle of Gettysburg was one of the last major battles of the war. More importantly, it was the beginning of the end for the Confederate cause.

General Robert E. Lee

Just like McClellan had done a year before, Mead refused to follow Lee as he retreated. Even though it took Lee almost a week to cross the river, Mead allowed Lee to escape back into Virginia. Lincoln was upset. He cried, "We had them within our grasp. I am distressed immeasurably because of it." Lincoln read Mead's telegraph where he boasted that he had been able to "drive the invader from our soil." Lincoln repeated, "Drive the invader from our soil! My God! Is that all?" Weeks after Gettysburg, Lincoln asked Mead, "Do you know, general, what your attitude towards Lee for a week after the battle reminded me of?" Mead replied, "No, Mr. President, what is it?" Lincoln said, "an old woman trying to shoo her geese across the creek."

During the three day battle, a total of 75,000 Confederate troops engaged 85,000 Union troops. Union casualties numbered more than 23,000 while Confederate causalities totaled more than 28,000. Mead's bloody experience at Gettysburg changed him. Contrary to earlier in the war, after Gettysburg Mead was never again able to launch an offensive. No matter what strategic plans he adopted, he ended up ordering his men to fall into defensive positions. While Lincoln waited for word on the siege on Vicksburg, he commented that if Grant was successful, he would depend on Grant "the rest of the war."

Fall of Vicksburg (July 4, 1863)

Congress and the press had grown impatient with the long siege of Vicksburg. However, Lincoln encouraged Grant not to loosen his "bulldog grip" on Vicksburg. Lincoln believed that Vicksburg had great strategic importance. He explained:

> Valuable as New Orleans (a port located at the mouth of the Mississippi River the opens at the Gulf of Mexico) [is], Vicksburg will be even more so. We may take all Northern ports of the Confederacy, and they can still defy us from Vicksburg. It means...a cotton country where they can raise staple without interference.

Vicksburg was the last major Confederate stronghold on the Mississippi. By the summer of 1863, control of Vicksburg would ensure control of the entire river. After about a month of defending the port, Confederate troops began to suffer serious food shortages. On July 3, the Confederate commander sent a message with a flag of truce to General Grant, who accepted Confederate surrender the next day. The fall of Vicksburg was a serious blow to the Confederate war effort. Jefferson Davis understood the importance of the loss calling Vicksburg the "nailhead that held the South's two halves together." In October 1863, Lincoln appointed Grant commander of the Departments of the Ohio, Cumberland, and Tennessee, making him the virtual head of all operations in the West.

New York City Draft Riots

Due to a need for more troops, on March 3, 1863 the U.S. Congress passed the Enrollment Act (or draft). It was the first time in American history that citizens were forced to join the military. The policy was extremely unpopular and was met with protests all across the nation. Since the policy was so unpopular, the government allowed for draftees the opportunity to pay $300 commutation fee in exchange for military service. In turn, the government used the money to pay bounties to encourage men to volunteer. Aside from being excused from service for medical reasons, draftees were also allowed to pay a substitute to serve in their place. Many poor Irishmen living in New York that could not afford to pay to get out of service resented what they called a "rich man's war, poor man's fight."

In the summer of 1863, draft riots broke out in New York City. Horatio Seymour, Governor of New York, was "tormented by the terrible reminiscence of the riots." Seymour informed John Hay that "the mob...aimed to destroy the great necessities of New York; light, water, & communication." Many rioters killed African Americans (including children) and burned down African American schools, businesses, and homes. According to Seymour, hundreds of people were killed and troops had to be called in to restore order.

Confederate Shortages and "Bread Riots"

Throughout the war, shortages of food and supplies were a constant problem in the South. However, the passage and enforcement of the Emancipation Proclamation resulted in greater shortages. As Union invading armies captured Southern territories, the Proclamation gave troops the right to liberate slaves. In addition, news of the Proclamation encouraged many slaves to escape to the North. Consequently, the South had fewer slaves to plant and harvest crops.

As storehouses and pantries became bare, desperation for the basic necessities of life drove some Southerners to take desperate measures. For example, an Atlanta, Georgia storekeeper reported that a woman "toting a gun, simply took food for her starving family when she had no money to pay." In 1863, starving Southerners headed to the Confederate capital in Richmond, Virginia for help. Finding no help, one woman complained, "We are starving. As soon as enough of us get together we are going to the bakeries and each of us will take a loaf of bread."

During four days in April, 1863, hundreds of hungry refugees (mostly women and children) stormed Richmond's local shops and took food from the shelves. Confederate troops were called to stop the thefts, but the crowd of hungry people refused to obey. Jefferson Davis spoke to the rioters in an attempt to calm them. However, he was met with ridicule. It was only after he promised to supply them with rations of rice that order was restored.

Lincoln's Vetoes Mead's Plans

In October, Mead sent Lincoln his plan to attack Richmond. Lincoln vetoed his plan. He wrote him explaining why he rejected the plan:

> To avoid misunderstanding, let me say that to attempt to fight the enemy slowly back into his entrenchments at Richmond and then to capture him, is an idea I have been trying to repudiate for quite a year. My judgment is so clear against it that I would scarcely allow the attempt to be made if the general in command should desire to make it.... I have constantly desired the Army of the Potomac to make Lee's army and not Richmond, its objective point. If our army cannot fall upon the enemy and hurt him where he is, it is plain to me it can gain nothing by attempting to follow him over a succession of entrenched lines into a fortified city.

Mead did not make the Confederate Army the target. He refused to give up his plan. In late October, Mead asked Lincoln for permission to move his base of operations to Fredericksburg where he could then launch an attack on Richmond. Lincoln again said no.

Gettysburg Address (November 19, 1863)

In July 1863, the North had gained two important victories: Gettysburg and Vicksburg. Months later, Lincoln was invited to make "a few appropriate remarks" at the dedication of a National Cemetery at Gettysburg. After three days of fighting at Gettysburg, Lee had retreated on the 4th of July – independence day. Lincoln saw a connection between July 4, 1776 (when the nation was declared free) and July 4, 1863 (which Lincoln called "a new birth of freedom").

Lincoln had always regarded the Declaration of Independence as being of the upmost importance. In his Address in Independence Hall (Philadelphia) two years earlier, Lincoln spoke about the principle of equality:

> I am filled with deep emotion at finding myself standing here, in this place, where collected together the wisdom, the patriotism, the devotion to principle, from which sprang the institutions under which we live.... I have never had a feeling politically that did not spring from the sentiments embodied in the Declaration of Independence.... It was not the mere matter of separation of the Colonies from the mother land; but that sentiment in the Declaration of Independence which gave liberty .... Now, my friends, can this country be saved upon that basis? If it can, I will consider myself one of the happiest men in the world.... If it cannot be saved upon that principle.... I would rather be assassinated on this spot than surrender it.

Lincoln accepted the invitation to speak at the Gettysburg ceremony, because he knew that it would be an appropriate opportunity to address the nation. He wanted to define what the war was all about in order to give the nation a reason to continue to fight until the war was won. There had been much bloodshed, misery, and loss, but Lincoln was to point out that the sacrifices were not in vain. They were for a greater good.

The old story that Lincoln dashed off the Address on the back of an envelope on his way to Gettysburg is a myth. Lincoln chose his words carefully and he meticulously planned the speech with a purpose. Lincoln left several re-written versions of the Address in which he scratched out words and added others with, sometimes, only slightly different connotations. He designed the Address for a purpose which went beyond the ceremony. He sought to preserve the Union by uniting the North under a common ground—the war effort.

On November 19, 1863, several speakers each took

their turn before the audience. In fact, Edward Everett, the featured speaker, spoke for two hours before it was Lincoln's turn to speak. Lincoln rose, delivered his short two-minute speech, and then sat back down before anyone had a chance to take his picture. John Russell Young from the Philadelphia press leaned over and asked Lincoln, "Is that all?" Lincoln answered, "Yes." Everett said, "It is not what I expected from him. I am disappointed." Ward Hill Lamon, Lincoln's body guard, said that it did "not impress [him] as one of his great speeches."

Abraham Lincoln, 1863

However, the reactions from people who had witnessed the oral presentation of the Address from just a few feet away was very different to reactions from people who read the Address in newspaper reports the next day. After reading the Address, Everett changed his initial assessment. He wrote Lincoln: "I should be glad if I could flatter myself that I came as near the central idea of the occasion in two hours as you did in two minutes." The editor of *Harper's Weekly* wrote, "The few words of the President were from the heart to the heart. They cannot be read…without kindly emotion." Weeks later, Lincoln received letters of praise for his Address from England. Today, it is regarded as one of the greatest American speeches.

Artist rendition of Lincoln delivering the Gettysburg Address

The Address helped civilian and military morale by pointing out the Gettysburg victory as an important advantage. However, the Address also did something revolutionary. In the Address, Lincoln defined the Declaration of Independence as the founding document of America. Speaking in 1863, he said, "For score and seven years ago (87 years ago) our fathers brought forth on this continent, a new nation…" referring to the Declaration of 1776 (which stressed liberty) and not the Constitution of 1787 (which protected slave property).

"The few words of the President were from the heart to the heart."

Once people read the Address and realized its implications, some people questioned the validity of Lincoln's interpretation. Lincoln later explained by quoting the Preamble and pointing out that the Constitution was "ordain[ed]" only "to form a more perfect Union." The Union, he argued, existed since the Declaration of Independence. The Address was also Lincoln's way of preparing the nation for the new and radical direction that the war had taken. A war that had begun due to economic, cultural, and political issues, had now been transformed into a war for freedom. Lincoln honored the men that gave their lives to advance the cause of liberty and the greater good. He also challenged the living to continue the work that the dead had begun. Otherwise, he said, the dead died "in vain."

Gettysburg Address

Four score and seven years ago our fathers brought forth on this continent, a new nation, conceived in Liberty, and dedicated to the proposition that all men are created equal.

Now we are engaged in a great civil war, testing whether that nation, or any nation so conceived and so dedicated, can long endure. We are met on a great battle-field of that war. We have come to dedicate a portion of that field, as a final resting place for those who here gave their lives that that nation might live. It is altogether fitting and proper that we should do this.

But, in a larger sense, we cannot dedicate—we cannot consecrate—we cannot hallow—this ground. The brave men, living and dead, who struggled here, have consecrated it, far above our poor power to add or detract. The world will little note, nor long remember what we say here, but it can never forget what they did here. It is for us the living, rather, to be dedicated here to the unfinished work which they who fought here have thus far so nobly advanced. It is rather for us to be here dedicated to the great task remaining before us—that from these honored dead we take increased devotion to that cause for which they gave the last full measure of devotion—that we here highly resolve that these dead shall not have died in vain—that this nation, under God, shall have a new birth of freedom—and that government of the people, by the people, for the people, shall not perish from the earth.

Note: This is the "Bliss Copy" of the speech, which is the most often reproduced version. However, other versions of the speech exist (Nicolay Copy, Hay Copy, Everett Copy, and Bancroft Copy). Each version contains minor variations.

Lincoln understood that, for some people, saving the Union was in "itself insufficient reason for the enormous sacrifices being demanded" of them. So, he put the matter on a higher plane. Lincoln declared the war to be a test to see if the concepts on which the country was founded on were true. Surely, Lincoln's approach in the Gettysburg Address was much more radical than his earlier war policies. In an attempt to bring the war to a close, he would take even more radical and destructive measures in 1864 and 1865.

CHAPTER 5

1864-1865

Total War

Total War may be understood as a war designed to destroy not only enemy troops, but also enemy goods and transportation routes. It is war against armies, the general population, and all enemy resources. In short, it is not just a war against the military, it is also a war against civilians. With the war dragging on into 1864, Lincoln appointed new kinds of generals who would be willing and able to wage total war on the South.

General William T. Sherman

New Kinds of Generals

Lincoln placed U.S. Grant in charge of the entire Union Army and William T. Sherman in command in Georgia. Unlike McClellan, both of these generals agreed with Lincoln's grand strategy of total war, and were very willing to carry it out. After the Battle of Shiloh, General Grant had also been convinced that only hard war would be able to bring down the rebellion. This, in Grant's view, included the freeing of the slaves. If the South "cannot be whipped in any other way than through a war against slavery," Grant wrote, "let it come to that." General Sherman was, perhaps, the strongest advocate and enforcer of hard war against the South. In his opinion, it was the duty of commanders to take rebel houses, fields, and kick people out of their homes, "helpless, to starve." Sherman reasoned that, "it may be wrong, but that [did not] alter the case." He believed his "duty [was] not to build up; it [was] rather to destroy the rebel army and whatever of wealth or property it had founded its boasted strength upon."

Grant and Sherman launched simultaneous attacks on both Confederate troops and civilians. They burned down buildings including homes, barns, and railroad stations. They destroyed telegraph wires and railroad tracks. They confiscated livestock to feed their troops, and they shot horses, cows, and pigs that they could not carry away with them. In the course of a few weeks, many Southern citizens lost their businesses, homes, and lives. Years after the war, Sherman was asked how he could wage such a destructive war against Southern Americans, and he responded, "War is Hell."

Tried by War

Lincoln was adamant about the new character of the war. He told Secretary of War Stanton that it was time to deliver "decisive and extensive blows." He affirmed that "the Administration must set an example, and strike at the heart of the rebellion." With emancipation in effect, there was now no way of reconciliation with the Confederacy. In Lincoln's view, it was now "an issue which [could] only be tried by war, and decided by victory."

Abraham Lincoln, 1864

General-in-Chief Grant

Shortly after Lincoln appointed Grant General-in-Chief, Lincoln called Grant into his office, took down a large map from the wall and instructed Grant on strategy. Lincoln wanted Grant to coordinate a multi-point offensive. This was the very thing that he had wanted McClellan to do years earlier, but had been refused because McClellan's training dictated a concentration of force in a single

General U.S. Grant, 1864

point. But, unlike McClellan, Grant did listen to Lincoln, and his movements gave the President much joy. John Hay recorded in his diary that Lincoln instructed Grant to use all of his men during battles: "Those not skinning can hold a leg." Grant liked this phrase so much that he often used it in his own telegrams.

With emancipation in effect, there was now no way of reconciliation with the Confederacy. In Lincoln's view, it was now "an issue which [could] only be tried by war, and decided by victory."

As General-in-Chief, Grant was dedicated to victory at any cost. During the Battle of the Wilderness (May 5-7, 1864) Grant and Lee faced off for the first time. Lee made plans to confront Grant's forces in the dense Virginia woods, which gave his 65,000 troops two major advantages. First, Lee's troops were familiar with the terrain. Second, the dense wilderness negated Grant's greater troop numbers (115,000). In spite of the disadvantages, Grant refused to retreat after two days of fighting and heavy casualties. In fact, Grant incurred even more casualties after he ordered his battered troops to pursue Lee's retreating army. By the end of the battle, Grant lost the most troops (17,666 Union causalities to 11,033 Confederate casualties). Due to Grant's willingness to wage costly aggressive war, Lee accused him of wanton murder of his own troops.

Grant also ordered a suspension of all prisoner of war

exchanges in order to prevent any increase in Southern forces. Bad conditions in prisoner of war camps coupled with Grant's refusal to exchange prisoners led directly to many atrocities at Andersonville and elsewhere. From Grant's and Lincoln's perspectives, these results (although regrettable) were necessary costs of war.

Fort Stevens

On July 11 and July 12, 1864 Confederate Major General Jubal Early made a push toward the capital. Union forces were able to stop his advance effectively. However, the military operation gained some fame, because of Lincoln's presence during the battle. Lincoln's appearances on battlefields fascinated the troops to such an extent that some fictional stories became popular.

For example, Lincoln visited Fort Stevens by carriage on both days to observe the Confederate attack. A story sprang up that Confederate sharpshooters took several shots at Lincoln. According to the story, while the bullets were whizzing past Lincoln's head someone in the fort yelled at him, "Get down, you damn fool!" Depending on the version of the story, either future Supreme Court Justice Oliver Wendell Holmes Jr., or Elizabeth Thomas (a nearby resident) or Union Major General Horatio Wright was responsible for reprimanding the president. The true story may never be known.

1864 Presidential Campaign: Republican Divisions

Lincoln saw very little hope in being re-elected in 1864. Even his own party was divided. In the Spring of 1864, reporter J. M. Minchell interviewed the president about "the great political question of the day"—the upcoming presidential election. At the time of the interview, Lincoln had not yet been nominated as the official Republican candidate. Attempts to make Secretary of the Treasury Salmon P. Chase the Republican candidate had "culminated in disaster;" Chase's supporters had backed down, because they feared Lincoln's political patronage.

After the attempt to nominate Chase as the Republican nominee failed, some Republicans began to support General John C. Fremont for the position. In fact, on May 31, 1864, some discontented Republicans held a secret convention in which they nominated Fremont. Fremont's father-in-law was Senator Thomas Hart Benton, one of the most powerful men in Congress. Fremont was at first encouraged by Benton's support, but Fremont withdrew from the race before the election. Some historians believe that Lincoln struck some sort of secret deal with Fremont.

Once Lincoln was chosen as the Republican candidate, he chose Andrew Johnson, a Southerner, as his vice presidential running mate. Lincoln's choice of Johnson was based on Lincoln's ability to plan for the future. After the war, the divided nation had to be reunited, and, Lincoln thought, a Southern vice president would be able to reach out to his countrymen at that crucial time.

Grant's Siege of Petersburg

Since Union troops had laid a siege on Petersburg for many months without victory, Lincoln sent a message of encouragement. He telegraphed Grant: "I have seen your dispatch expressing your unwillingness to break your hold where you are. Neither am I willing. Hold on with a bull-dog grip, and chew & choke, as much as possible."

Lincoln was much pleased with Grant's tenacity for his task. Once asked about his regard for Grant as a general, Lincoln answered that Grant had "the *gift* of a bull-dog! Once let him get his teeth *in*, and nothing can shake him off." Lincoln and Grant worked well together because they agreed on the course the war should take, but Lincoln still remained the chief architect of war strategy. Lincoln gave Grant permission to continue to hold Petersburg until it fell in April, 1865.

Sherman Sets his sights on Atlanta, Georgia

General Sherman has been credited for being the first American general to wage Total War. During his Atlanta Campaign, Savannah Campaign ("March to the Sea"), and Carolina Campaign Sherman marched through Atlanta and South Carolina demolishing railroads, bridges, cutting telegraph lines, burning farms, seizing produce and livestock to feed his army, and reducing the South's work force by liberating slaves.

On September 4, 1864, Sherman evacuated Atlanta. A woman recalled, "He issued an order exiling the citizens. We were all sent out...we were turned out in the woods like cattle." After the forced evacuation of Atlanta residents, Sherman ordered that all military outposts and supplies be burned. The fires spread quickly and soon much of Atlanta burned to the ground.

1864 Presidential Campaign: The Democrats

On September 6, 1864, Reporter J. P. Thompson interviewed Lincoln at the White House. Thompson congratulated Lincoln on the capture of Atlanta. Lincoln responded by adding that more military victories were needed in order to insure reelection. In Lincoln's view, his re-election was necessary in order to insure the preservation of the Union. The Democratic Party was heavily influenced by the Peace Platform to bring the war to an end at all cost, even if the Union was still divided.

The political situation grew worse when it was discovered that plans were under way for running one of Lincoln's former generals, George Gordon Mead, for president. But, eventually the Democrats chose George B. McClellan ("Little Mac"), another one of Lincoln's generals, instead. Thompson reassured Lincoln that McClellan had not yet accepted the Democratic Peace Platform. Thompson recalled, "I observed that [McClellan] seemed about as slow in getting upon the platform as he was in taking Richmond." With a twinkle in his eye, Lincoln responded, "I think he must be *entrenching*."

According to Thompson, at this point, Lincoln became serious and assessed McClellan's character. In Thompson's opinion, "there was no maliciousness in his tone, no trace of personal rivalry or animosity. It was the utterance of a deliberate judgment." "Well," said Lincoln, "he doesn't know yet whether he will accept or decline. And he never will know. Somebody must do it for him. For of all the men I have had to do with in my life, indecision is most strongly marked in General McClellan; if that can be said to be strong which is the essence of weakness."

However, McClellan eventually did embrace the platform. He called the war a failure and promised its immediate end by negotiating agreeable peace terms with the South. Lincoln believed that McClellan's election would equate to Confederate victory and independence.

1864 Presidential Election: Lincoln

Lincoln granted soldiers leave from service so that they had the opportunity to vote. News from Atlanta, other fronts (including the Shenandoah Campaign), and the military votes secured Lincoln his reelection in November. In the election, 116,887 soldiers voted for Lincoln while only 33,748 voted for McClellan. Lincoln also got more popular votes in 22 out of 25 states.

Above all, Lincoln's re-election hurt morale in the South. Confederate leaders knew that Lincoln would not compromise on his desire for Union, which meant at least four more years of war. By 1864, most Southerners no longer had the resources, manpower, or will to fight.

Sherman's March to the Sea

After Sherman captured Atlanta, he headed across Georgia destroying everything in his path. Savannah, Georgia was one of the few major Confederate ports still in operation. On December 22, 1864, Sherman wired Lincoln with the message, "I beg to present you, as a Christmas gift, the city of Savannah, with 150 heavy guns and plenty of ammunition, and also about 25,000 bales of cotton." Lincoln answered Sherman, "Many, many thanks for your Christmas gift, the capture of Savannah."

Almost at the Finish Line

By the end of 1864, under Grant's leadership, the West was securely under Union control. Sherman had destroyed supply lines and morale by waging Total War on the Deep South. After 1864, shortages would become much more acute for the South. In spite of diminishing resources, many Confederate Generals and soldiers were determined to continue fighting. But, within four months, the hard hand of war would bring the war to a close.

Lincoln's Second Inaugural Address (March 4, 1865)

As the war was drawing to a close, Lincoln began making Reconstruction plans. He revealed the tone that he intended to take toward the South in the coming months and

Vol. IX.—No. 429.]   NEW YORK, SATURDAY, MARCH 18, 1865.

LINCOLN TAKING THE OATH AT HIS SECOND INAUGURATION, March 4, 1865.—Photographed by Gardner, Washington.—[See

Lincoln's Second Inauguration

years. He said that Reconstruction would be conducted, "With malice toward none; with charity for all…to bind up the nation's wounds; to care for him who shall have borne the battle, and for his widow, and his orphan--to do all which may achieve and cherish a just and lasting peace, among ourselves, and with all nations."

Fall of Richmond (April 1865)

Lincoln never took his hands out of the war. For example, he visited with his top generals in the field to discuss strategy shortly before Richmond fell. Captain John S. Barnes of the U.S.S. *Bat* escorted Lincoln from Washington to Richmond in 1865. Upon reaching Grant, Lincoln ordered an official review of his troops. At Grant's headquarters, Lincoln heard news of an ensuing serious battle at Petersburg, and he "expressed a great desire to visit the scene of the action." He was taken to the scene by train. The battle was still going on when they arrived. "The ground immediately about us," wrote Barnes, "was still strewn with dead and wounded men, Federal and Confederate. Firing of both musketry and artillery was seen and heard." Lincoln then rode on horseback to an "eminence nearby, from which a good view of the scene could be secured."

On April 3, 1865, Stanton telegraphed Lincoln and protested the President's actions in "exposing himself" to battlefield dangers. Stanton was critical of Lincoln's risks and drew "contrasts between the duty of a general and a president," but Lincoln answered that he had been to Petersburg and would next be visiting Richmond. By this point in time everyone at Grant's headquarters "seemed confident that Petersburg would soon fall and with it Richmond," since, "Sherman would be coming up victoriously from the South and uniting with Grant's army." To Lincoln's delight, it also seemed to all that the end of the war was not far off.

President Lincoln, Generals Grant, Sherman, Sheridan, Mead, several others, and Admiral Porter all gathered at Grant's headquarters to discuss war strategy. The next day Sherman returned to his army. Grant received a dispatch

President Lincoln at General Grant's Headquarters

announcing that Petersburg was evacuated and that Union troops were in possession of it. The day after that, Grant received a telegraph confirming a "rumor which had reached Grant at Petersburg, that Richmond was being evacuated and that General Lee was in retreat and President Davis had fled."

After capturing Richmond, Union troops began destroying the rebel ironclads and setting the city on fire. When Lincoln arrived, Richmond was still "in flames, dense masses of smoke resting over the city." Slaves were everywhere, and, when they found out that the tall man was Lincoln, they crowded around him. Barnes recorded the scene at Richmond:

> It was a scene of indescribable confusion. Confederate bonds of the denomination of $1,000 were scattered about on the grass,

bundles of public papers and documents littered the floors, chairs and desks were upset, with every evidence of hasty abandonment and subsequent looting.

Lincoln in Richmond, Virginia

The supreme moment for Barnes of the whole Richmond affair was when Lincoln visited the Confederate White House:

The President entered by the front door....He was then led into a room...which had been Mr. Davis's reception room and office....Mr. Lincoln walked across the room to the easy chair and sank down in it. A few of us were gathered about the door; little was said by anyone. It was a supreme moment--the home of the fleeing President of the Confederacy invaded by his opponents after years of bloody contests for its possession, and now occupied by the President of the United States, Abraham Lincoln, seated in the chair almost warm from the pressure of the body of Jefferson Davis!

Although President Davis remained at large by this date, Lee's surrender to Grant at Appomattox Courthouse, Virginia on April 9 struck a mortal blow to the rebellion. Lincoln was assassinated five days after Lee's surrender.

CONCLUSION

Union and Secession

While Confederate leaders and even some northerners clamored for Confederate independence, Lincoln would not let the rebelling states go. He would not recognize secession for several reasons. On an international level, a divided nation left a weaker military presence. The raw force of economics also had to be considered. After all, it was no secret that Northern factories were dependent on the South's raw materials. However, the most important facet of the contemplated "divorce" between North and South was political in nature. Lincoln believed that, as president, it was his responsibility to preserve the Union. More importantly, he believed that if just one state was allowed to secede, it would be just a matter of time before the rest of the Union unraveled.

Other theories about the nature of Union existed. One theory was based on the constitutional doctrine of state sovereignty. According to this view, since states entered the Union voluntarily by state conventions, they could leave the Union in the same way. In fact, the threat of secession was nothing new in 1860. During the War of 1812, New Englanders suffering from economic sanctions were the first to threaten the federal government with secession unless they were given some relief. Also, in 1828, South Carolina planters protested the Tariff of 1828 by threatening to nullify, or choose not to obey, federal laws that hurt its interests. The threat of nullification led to a debate in Congress. President Andrew Jackson threatened to send troops to enforce federal law, but the nullification crisis was mostly subdued by a congressional compromise tariff in 1833.

Another more narrow view of the right to secession stated that Texas, which had been a sovereign nation before it was annexed into the United States, and the original 13 states that signed the Declaration of Independence in 1776 had the right to secede. On the other hand, none of the other states in the Union could claim this right, because the federal government had created them all from government owned lands.

However, Lincoln disagreed with these and any other theories of secession. In his view, no state had the right to secede. During the secession crisis, Lincoln was unmovable. Inseparable Union was an obsession with him. In his First Inaugural Address, on March 4, 1861, he stated that he understood the Constitution to make the Union of the states perpetual. In his view, no government had ever created the means for its own disintegration. He stated that disunion would contradict the Constitution that he was bound to uphold. Consequently, even during the secession crisis, he stated that the Union must remain unbroken. Furthermore, he did not recognize the Confederate States of America, but, rather, he often referred to them as rebels or Union states that were temporarily in rebellion. Ultimately, Lincoln's conviction to wage a costly war to preserve the Union, served to give his view of the nature of Union greater weight over all others.

Heritage of Emancipation

For Lincoln the war was not about slavery. Lincoln did not oppose slavery where it already existed. In fact, in spite of his personal feelings against slavery, he was convinced that the president was politically powerless when it came to slavery. Even after he later justified emancipation as a "military necessity," he did so as a means to an end. Unlike the political aspects of Union, to Lincoln slavery was negotiable. He would free all slaves if it would save the Union, or he would free no slaves if it would save the Union. Slavery was merely a bargaining chip in late 1862. In contrast, the preservation of the Union was the coveted prize.

In early 1863, Lincoln transformed the war into a struggle against human bondage. The Emancipation Proclamation was an obvious sign post of Lincoln's change in strategies. It served as both a diplomatic and military weapon. As a diplomatic weapon, the Proclamation kept European nations out of the war. Left to fend for itself, the Confederacy was doomed in the face of a much more populous and industrialized North. As a military weapon, it robbed the Confederacy of the support system that slaves had provided. In addition, Lincoln's decision to allow freed slaves and free blacks to join the Union military transformed the nation forever. Although this move was primarily meant to address military needs, Lincoln realized that he could not ask freedmen to fight only to tell them later that they were not citizens of the nation they fought for. So, although the Proclamation only freed slaves in the rebelling states (beginning on January 1, 1863), after the war it led to universal freedom (Thirteenth Amendment, 1865).

But, what legal status would freedmen have in post-war American society? After Lincoln's assassination, Congress answered these questions by granting former slaves citizenship status (Fourteenth Amendment, 1868) and by granting all male African American citizens the right to vote (Fifteenth Amendment, 1870). Both of these Reconstruction Amendments were passed to address pressing issues of that time, but these laws had far-reaching effects. Although the Fifteenth Amendment did not apply to women, it served as a model for the Women's Suffrage Movement before and after its passage. Under the provisions of the Fourteenth Amendment, since 1868 people of all races born or naturalized in the United States have been granted citizenship (with equal protection of life, liberty, and property under the law). Even though Lincoln's Proclamation did not encompass rights specified in the Reconstruction Amendments, it did set the stage for them, and it made the nation's multi-racial future inevitable.

The Backwoods Jupiter

Lincoln was a war president. At first, Lincoln waged a limited war with the hope that the loyal citizens of the rebel states would influence a return to the Union. He also did not wish to destroy the South's means of production and transportation, which were so necessary for Northern factories and hence for the economic life of the reunified country Lincoln envisioned. But, when Southern resistance stiffened and a quick and peaceful solution to the secession crisis did not emerge, he became convinced that only hard war could bring back Union. Eventually the war would degenerate into a completely barbarous struggle (Total War) that did not discriminate between soldiers and civilians. Property was taken and burned. Slaves were set free and used against the South. In essence, Lincoln destroyed the

South's economic, social, and political institutions with no regard for life or limb.

Although Lincoln is one of the most well-known American presidents, he may also be one of the least well understood. Ever since his death, biographers have continually re-crafted Lincoln's image and have come to widely divergent conclusions about him. This is particularly true of his role as a strategist in the face of the nation's Civil War.

How could the statesman-like Lincoln who demanded a soft approach to war early on become the callous Lincoln who later waged Total War? How could the humanitarian Lincoln who pledged "malice toward none" and "charity toward all" in his Second Inaugural Address justify war against Southern civilians? How could a president who pledged not to abolish slavery end up freeing slaves? Such apparently contradictory tendencies have led historians to characterize Lincoln as everything from the "Great Emancipator" to a racist tyrant.

The answer to these questions lies in Lincoln's obsession with Union. The reunification of the nation was his main goal while many other things were negotiable. Thus Lincoln the politician and Lincoln the general were one-in-the-same, and it is only when this fundamental truth about the man is considered that his military decision-making can be understood. Far from making tactically inept decisions, Lincoln made strategic masterstrokes that continually channeled the forces of war in the direction he deemed necessary. And in the end, he was successful.

While perhaps the popularly perceived "Great Emancipator" image may not be the most accurate view of Lincoln, it does seem safe to conclude that he was the Savior of the Union. With a steady hand on operational military strategy, Lincoln's vision of grand strategy ultimately determined the outcome of the Civil War. Lincoln was, in-deed, a master political and military strategist. Like a "backwoods Jupiter," he skillfully "wield[ed] the bolts of war."

BIBLIOGRAPHY

Primary Sources: Books

Abraham Lincoln Papers. Library of Congress. 3 Series. 97 Reels. (Also online at https://memory.loc.gov /ammem/alhtml/malhome.html)

Barnes, James J. and Patience P. Barnes, editors. *Private and Confidential Letters from British Ministers in Washington to the Foreign Secretaries in London, 1844-67.* London: Associated University Press, 1993.

Basler, Roy P., editor. *The Collected Works of Abraham Lincoln.* (9 Vols.). New Jersey: Rutgers University Press, 1953-1955.

Bates, David Homer. *Lincoln in the Telegraph Office.* New York: Century Co., 1907.

Brooks, Noah. *Washington in Lincoln's Time.* New York: Reinhart and Company, 1895.

Browning, Orville Hickman. *The Diary of Orville Hickman Browning.* (2 Vols.). Edited by Theodore C. Pease & James G. Randall. Ill.: Illinois State Historical Library, 1933.

Carpenter, F. B. *Six Month at the White House with Abraham Lincoln.* New York: Hurd and Houghton. 1866.

Dennet, Tyler, editor. *Lincoln and the Civil War in the Diaries and Letters of John Hay.* New York: Dodd, Mead & Company, 1939.

Ferri-Pisani, Lieutenant-Colonel Cammille. *Prince Napoleon in America, 1861; Letters from His Aid-de-Camp.* Translated by Georges J. Joyaux. Bloomington: Indiana University Press, 1959.

Ford, Worthington Chauncy, editor. *A Cycle of Adams Letters, 1861-1865.* New York: Houghton Mifflin Co., 1920.

Herndon, William H. and Jesse W. Weik. *Herndon's Lincoln: The True Story of a Great Life.* 3 vols. Chicago: Clarke and Company, 1889.

Holzer, Harold, editor. *Dear Mr. Lincoln: Letters to the President.* Reading, Massachusetts: Addison-Wesley Publishing Company, 1995.

Long, E. B., ed. *Personal Memoirs of U. S. Grant.* New York: Da Capo Press, 1982.

McClellan, General George B. *McClellan's Own Story: The War for the Union, the Soldiers Who Fought It, the Civilians Who Directed It, and His Relationship to It and to Them.* New York: Charles L. Webster and Co., 1887.

McClure, Alexander. *Abraham Lincoln and Men of War-Times: Some Personal Recollections of War and Politics During the Lincoln Administration.* Philadelphia Times Publishing, 1892.

Mearns, David C., ed. *The Lincoln Papers.* New York: Doubleday & Company, Inc., 1948.

Niven, John., ed. *The Salmon P. Chase Papers.* (4 Vols.). Kent, Ohio: The Kent State University Press, 1997.

Rice, Allen Thorndike, editor. *Reminiscences of Abraham Lincoln by Distinguished Men of His Time.* New York: Harper and Brothers, 1886.

Russell, William Howard. *My Diary North and South.* Boston: T. O. H. P. Burnham, 1863.

Sears, Stephen W., ed. *The Civil War Papers of George B. McClellan: Selected Correspondence 1860-1865.* New York: Da Capo Press, 1992.

Simon, John Y., ed. *The Papers of Ulysses S. Grant.* (16 Vols.). Carbondale, Ill., 1967-1995.

Stoddard, William O. *Inside the White House in War Times.* New York: Charles L. Webster & Co., 1890.

Strong, George Templeton. *The Diary of the Civil War, 1860-1865.* Edited by Allen Nevins. New York: The Macmillan Company, 1962.

Wolseley, Field Marshall Viscount. *The American Civil War: An English View.* Edited by James a Rawley. Charlottesville: The University of Virginia, 1964.

Primary Source: CD-ROM
The War of the Rebellion: A Compilation of the Official Records of the Union and Confederate Armies. [CD-ROM] (Carmel, Indiana: Guild Press of Indiana, Inc., 1996).

Primary Sources: Newspapers and Magazines
Anti-Slavery Reporter
Atlantic Monthly
Appleton's Magazine
Charleston Mercury
Congregationalist
Galaxy
Harper's Weekly
London Daily News
London Punch
London Spectator
London Times
Manchester Guardian
New York Times
New York Tribune
Richmond Enquirer

Secondary Sources: Books
Ballard, Colin R. *The Military Genius of Abraham Lincoln.* London: Oxford University Press, 1926.

Baily, Thomas A. *A Diplomatic History of the American People.* New York: F.S. Crofts & Co., 1946.

Beard, Charles A. and Mary R. Bread. *The Rise of American Civilization.* 2 vols. New York: The MacMillan Company, 1930.

Boritt, Gabor S., ed. *Lincoln, the War President.* New York: Oxford University Press, 1992.

Boritt, Gabor S. *The Gettysburg Gospel: The Lincoln Speech Nobody Knows.* Simon and Schuster, 2006.

Bruce, Robert V. *Lincoln and the Tools of War.* Indianapolis and New York: The Bobbs-Merrill Company, Inc., 1956.

Current, Robert N. *The Lincoln Nobody Knows.* Westport, Connecticut: Greenwood Press, 1958.

Donaldson, Jordan and Edwin J. Pratt. *Europe and the American Civil War.* Boston, 1931.

Franklin, John Hope. *The Emancipation Proclamation.* New York: Doubleday & Co., Inc., 1963.

Gienapp, William E. *Abraham Lincoln and the American Political Tradition.* Edited by John L. Thomas. Amherst: The University of Massachusetts Press, 1986.

Guelzo, Allen C. *Lincoln's Emancipation Proclamation: The End of Slavery in America.* New York: Simon and Schuster, 2004.

Hagerman, Edward. *The American Civil War and the Origins of Modern Warfare: Ideas, Organization and Field Command.* Bloomington, Indianapolis: Indiana University Press, 1988.

Harper, Robert S. *Lincoln and the Press.* New York: McGraw-Hill Book Company, Inc., 1951.

Hassler, Warren W., Jr. *General George B. McClellan, Shield of the Union.* Baton Rouge: Louisiana State University Press, 1957.

Jenkins, Brian. *Britain & the War for Union.* London: McGill-Queen's University Press, 1974.

Litwack, Leon F. *North of Slavery: The Negro in the Free States, 1790-1860.* Chicago: University of Chicago Press, 1961.

Long, E. B. and Barbara Long. *The Civil War Day by Day: An Almanac 1861-1865.* New York: Da Capo Press, 1985.

Luvaas, Jay. *The Military Legacy of the Civil War: The European Inheritance.* Chicago: The University of Chicago Press, 1959.

Maurice, Sir Frederick. *Statesmen and Soldiers of the Civil War.* Boston: Little Brown and Co., 1926.

McPherson, James M. *Abraham Lincoln and the Second American Revolution.* New York: Oxford University Press, 1991.

_____. *Battle Cry of Freedom.* New York: Oxford University Press, 1988.

_____. *For Cause and Comrades: Why Men Fought in the Civil War.* New York: Oxford University Press, 1977.

_____. *Tried by War: Abraham Lincoln as Commander in Chief.* New York: The Penguin Press, 2008.

Michie, Peter S. *General McClellan*. New York: Great Commanders Series, 1901.

Miers, Earl S. *Lincoln Day by Day: A Chronology, 1809-1865*. 2nd Edition. Morningside Bookshop, 1988.

Monaghan, Jay. *Diplomat in Carpet Slippers: Abraham Lincoln Deals with Foreign Affairs*. Bobbs-Merrill Company, 1945.

Neely, Mark E., Jr. *The Abraham Lincoln Encyclopedia*. New York: Da Capo Press, 1984.

_____. The Fate of Liberty: Abraham Lincoln and Civil Liberties. New York: Oxford University Press, 1991.

Paludan, Philip Shaw. *The Presidency of Abraham Lincoln*. Lawrence: University of Kansas Press, 1994.

Pettet, Geoffrey. *Lincoln's War: The Untold Story of America's Greatest President as Commander in Chief*. New York: Random House, 2004.

Quarles, Benjamin. *Lincoln and the Negro*. New York: Da Capo, 1990.

Randall, James G. *Lincoln the President*. (2 vols.). New York: Dodd, Mead, 1945-1955.

White, Ronald C. *Lincoln's Greatest Speech: The Second Inaugural*. Simon and Schuster, 2002.

Wiley, Bell Irving. *The Life of Billy Yank*. Indianapolis, 1939.

Williams, Kenneth P. *Lincoln Finds a General: A Military Study of the Civil War*. (5 vols.). New York: Macmillan Co., 1949-1959.

Williams, T. Harry. *Lincoln and His Generals*. New York: Alfred A.Knopf, 1952.

Wills, Gary. *Lincoln at Gettysburg: The Words that Remade America*. New York: Simon & Schuster, 1992.

Woodham-Smith, Cecil. *Queen Victoria*. New York: Alfred A. Knopf, 1973.

INDEX

PHOTO CREDITS

All images are from the Library of Congress, in the public domain, with no known restrictions on publication.

Book Cover
(Front and back cover) Abraham Lincoln, Library of Congress, Prints & Photographs Division, [LC-DIG-highsm-12410 (digital file from original) LC-HS503-1149 (color film transparency)]

Chapter 1
(Page 4) Cotton gin, Library of Congress, Prints & Photographs Division, [LC-DIG-npcc-20403 (digital file from original)]
(Page 6) William Lloyd Garrison, Library of Congress, Prints & Photographs Division, [LC-USZ62-10320 (b&w film copy neg.)]
(Page 7) Sojourner Truth, Library of Congress, Prints & Photographs Division, [LC-USZ62-119343 (b&w film copy neg.)]
(Page 10) Harriet Tubman, Library of Congress, Prints & Photo-

graphs Division, [LC-USZ62-7816 (b&w film copy neg.)]
(Page 8) Frederick Douglass, Library of Congress, Prints & Photographs Division, [LC-USZ62-24165 (b&w film copy neg.)]
(Page 11) Abraham Lincoln, Library of Congress, Prints & Photographs Division, [LC-USZ62-4377 (b&w film copy neg. made from old photographic print)]
(Page 19) Stephen Douglas, Library of Congress, Prints & Photographs Division, [LC-DIG-cwpbh-00881 (digital file from original neg.)]
(Page 21) John Brown, Library of Congress, Prints & Photographs Division, [LC-USZ62-2472 (b&w film copy neg.)]

Chapter 2
(Page 26) Fort Sumter, Library of Congress, Prints & Photographs Division, [LC-DIG-ppmsca-35206 (digital file from original item, bottom left)]
(Page 29) Abraham Lincoln, Library of Congress, Prints & Photographs Division, [LC-USZ62-37402 (b&w film copy neg.)]
(Page 31) Jefferson Davis, Library of Congress, Prints & Photographs Division, [LC-DIG-cwpbh-00879 (digital file from original neg.)]
(Page 41) Scott's Great Snake [Library of Congress – no reproduction number]
(Page 42) Winfield Scott, Library of Congress, Prints & Photographs Division, [LC-USZ61-7 (b&w film copy neg.)]
(Page 47) George B. McClellan, Library of Congress, Prints & Photographs Division, [LC-DIG-ppmsca-33064 (digital file from original photograph)]

Chapter 3
(Page 53) U.S. Grant, Library of Congress, Prints & Photographs Division, [LC-DIG-cwpb-06941 (digital file from original neg.)]
(Page 56) George B. McClellan, Library of Congress, Prints & Photographs Division, [LC-USZ62-100750 (b&w film copy neg.)]
(Page 57) McClellan and May Ellen, his wife, Library of Congress, Prints & Photographs Division, [LC-DIG-cwpb-05665 (digital file from original neg.)]
(Page 66) Lincoln and McClellan at Antietam, Library of Congress, Prints & Photographs Division, [LC-B8171-7948 (b&w film

neg.)]
(Page 69) Henry W. Halleck, Library of Congress, Prints & Photographs Division, [LC-USZ62-128580 (b&w film copy neg.)]
(Page 64) Horace Greeley, Library of Congress, Prints & Photographs Division, [LC-USZ62-47450 (b&w film copy neg.)]

Chapter 4

(Page 74) Abraham Lincoln, Library of Congress, Prints & Photo-
graphs Division, [LC-DIG-ppmsca-19208 (digital file from orig-
inal)]
(Page 77) Abraham Lincoln, Library of Congress, Prints & Photo-
graphs Division, [LC-USZ62-61374 (b&w film copy neg.)]
(Page 81) African American Union Troops, Library of Congress,
Prints & Photographs Division, [LC-B8171-7890 (b&w film
neg.)]
(Page 82) Joseph Hooker, Library of Congress, Prints & Photographs
Division, [LC-USZ62-111519 (b&w film copy neg.)]
(Page 85) Robert E. Lee, Library of Congress, Prints & Photographs
Division, [LC-DIG-cwpbh-03116 (digital file from original neg.)]
(Page 91) Abraham Lincoln, Library of Congress, Prints & Photo-
graphs Division, [LC-DIG-ds-07061]
(Page 92) Gettysburg Address, Library of Congress, Prints & Photo-
graphs Division, [LC-USZ62-2006 (b&w film copy neg.)]

Chapter 5

(Page 97) William T. Sherman, Library of Congress, Prints & Photographs Division, [LC-B8172-6454 (b&w film neg.)]
(Page 99) Abraham Lincoln, Library of Congress, Prints & Photographs Division, [LC-USZ62-8120 (b&w film copy neg.)]
(Page 100) U.S. Grant, Library of Congress, Prints & Photographs
Division, [LC-DIG-ppmsca-35236 (digital file from original
item)]
(Page 107) Second Inaugural, Library of Congress, Prints & Photographs Division, [LC-USZ62-2578 (b&w film copy neg.)]
(Page 109) President Lincoln at General Grant's Headquarters, Library of Congress, Prints & Photographs Division, [LC-DIG-
pga-04980 (digital file from original item)]
(Page 110) Lincoln in Richmond, Library of Congress, Prints & Photographs Division, [LC-USZ62-6931 (b&w film copy neg.)]

ABOUT THE AUTHOR

Rolando Avila was born and raised in South Texas. He earned a Bachelor of Arts degree in History (1994), a Master of Arts degree in History (1999), and a Doctorate in Education (2013) from the University of Texas-Pan American. Avila is Lecturer of History at the University of Texas Rio Grande Valley (UTRGV). He has published many Civil War related articles and book chapters. In 2016, he made a presentation for UTRGV's Community History Archeology Project with Schools (CHAPS) Program in McAllen, Texas titled, "The Study of Local History and the Rio Grande Valley Civil War Trail." His most recent book is *Rio Grande Valley Civil War Trail: 40 Lesson Plans* (2017). For more information on the Rio Grande Valley Civil War Trail, please consult www.utrgv.edu/civilwar-trail/